CONSTITUTIONALISM
★ ★ ★ AND RIGHTS ★ ★ ★

CONSTITUTIONALISM
★★★ AND RIGHTS ★★★

EDITED BY

Gary C. Bryner and Noel B. Reynolds

BRIGHAM YOUNG UNIVERSITY

Library of Congress Cataloging-in-Publication Data
Bryner, Gary C. and Noel B. Reynolds
Constitutionalism and rights.

   "Four invited essays were originally presented in January of 1985 as a lecture series
inaugurating the celebration of the Bicentennial of the Constitution of the United
States of America at Brigham Young University"—Intro.
   Includes index.
   Contents: Constitutionalism and the politics of rights/by Gary C. Bryner—The
uncertain quest for welfare rights/by Richard A. Epstein—The "new" science of poli-
tics and constitutional government/by Walter Berns—[etc.]
   1. Civil rights—United States.   2. United States—
Constitutional law.   I. Bryner, Gary C., 1951–   II. Reynolds, Noel B.
Kf4749.A2C63 1987   323.4'0973   86-23272
ISBN 88-706-657-7

Brigham Young University, Provo, Utah 84602

Distributed by State University of New York Press,
State University Plaza, Albany, New York
12446-0001

Contents

Introduction

I t is fortuitous that the bicentennial celebrations of the writing
of the American Constitution are coming on the scene at a time
when historical and philosophical scholarship have begun to improve dramatically our ability to understand and appreciate that
great eighteenth-century achievement. This development is dou-
bly fortunate today because fundamental questions about how the
Constitution might be strengthened or revised are increasingly
being raised in our legislatures and public discussions. If we are to
build wisely on the heritage of the past as we undertake to make
adjustments for the future, it is imperative that we fully understand the reasons for our system's successes and failures. This
volume of essays and the lecture series from which it is mostly
drawn have been conceived as a contribution to that improved
understanding.

In contrast to the eighteenth-century Founders, today we ordinarily approach discussions of the Constitution through the concept of rights. But rights have become controversial. New tech-
nologies and social arrangements raise difficult questions about
rights that were unknown or unquestioned in that earlier day.
The volume begins with a systematic discussion of the notion of
rights and with careful attention to the development of that
concept over the last two centuries. In this introductory essay
Gary Bryner emphasizes an account of the contemporary debates
about rights and raises several questions that must be answered if
we are to make further progress in these discussions. Much more
attention, he argues, needs to be given to the mechanisms and
structures and procedures that can assure rights in a large bureaucratic state. Particularly important here is a consideration of the
paradox that increasing governmental powers in the pursuit of

rights may also serve to threaten other rights. Much of the debate that takes place in the name of rights would be better undertaken as a discussion of public choices and priorities that cannot be deduced from the Constitution, but, rather, reflect a willingness to pursue public policies on a more tentative basis.

Our second essayist focuses his attention on one of the newest and most controversial rights concepts as it arises in debates over public welfare programs. Richard Epstein undertakes to explain why it is that the quest for welfare rights has been (and will continue to be) so uncertain. Noting that we have no developed theory of rights to justify the massive welfare schemes of western democracies, he examines some recent attempts to develop such a theory and then goes on to explore the range of logically available alternative strategies. Epstein insists that theorists must recognize the responsibility to assess actual resources in any scheme of welfare rights. The inquiry reveals both a fundamental incompatibility between traditional common law and welfare rights and the fact that economic theory provides no reason to hope that welfare transfer schemes can possibly improve the economic condition of even the poor over the long run. Epstein does finally find one unexpected, second-level justification for welfare expenditures in the fact that much government regulation of capital and labor works against the poor as a public version of the tort of "interfering with prospective advantage." Though he recognizes the inadequate fit between this justification and present welfare schemes, he sees in it at least some substantial justification for a gradualist approach to reducing welfare programs while expanding the economic freedom of the poor.

The modern tendency to see a constitution as a longer version of a bill of abstract rights is quite at odds with the institutional balancing approach to constitutionalism that dominated eighteenth-century thought in America. Walter Berns shows us in his essay on the "new science of politics" that the crucial concepts in the American approach to a constitution were innovations designed to achieve "constitutional or limited government" as the primary means of securing individual freedom. The Americans distinguished themselves as the great generation of constitutionalists in the way they developed and integrated their ideas of representation, the protection of property, the desirability of a large commercial republic as opposed to a smaller classical republic, and the securing of rights to all persons equally.

This broader notion of constitutionalism, together with the beliefs from which it was derived, are the subject of the fourth essay. Noel Reynolds sees a need to redress the loss of constitutional wisdom in our generation. He surveys important historical examples of free societies, including some examples of primitive societies, to argue that freedom comes through constitutional balancing of political institutions and functions, and that freedom consists in the rule of law as protected by such balancing. Reynolds claims that the American constitutional experiment was the most successful precisely because it concentrated exclusively on the problem of protecting rule of law through institutional balancing and did not succumb to the temptation to implement moral truth, as did many of its less successful imitators. Reynolds concludes paradoxically that the political constitution which avoids moralistic pronouncements and emphasizes institutional arrangements will provide more freedom to individuals and groups to pursue their own moral ideals. And he explains that it is the limited altruism and intellectual capacity of men generally which dictates that this morally less-ambitious approach to human freedom and justice will always produce the best results. Reynolds further argues that freedom through rule of law and constitutionalism is only possible in a society in which the political culture strongly supports such institutions, inducing the citizenry to give of themselves for the protection and maintenance of their political institutions.

This last theme becomes the subject of the fifth essay. Thomas Pangle explicates the classical doctrine of republican virtue as a means of demonstrating how important public virtue—a political culture that encourages fraternity and self-sacrifice for the common good and the protection of the liberties of all citizens—is for a free society under constitutional government. He argues that the Founders of the new American nation clearly understood this and emphasized repeatedly the importance of the "general spirit of the people," their "manners and principles," their desire to pursue "the common good of the people" as preconditions for successful republican government. He further compares the views of the ancient Greeks with those of Madison and Jefferson and

3

others to highlight American innovations on this subject. This comparison leaves Pangle with a doubt as to whether the American Founders gave sufficient attention to the necessity of continually nurturing the public virtue that was so essential for the kind of republic they sought to create.

Michael Sandel's concluding essay steps back from all these specific issues and draws together some of the beginning and ending themes. Picking up on the older idea of "civic republicanism," he argues that contemporary emphasis on rights is a potentially dangerous development of modern liberalism. He outlines the differences between a "politics of rights," defended by liberals as an emphasis on individualism and individual rights, and a "politics of the common good," a view that champions community values and citizenship. Sandel sketches an interpretation of American history in which there is a transition from the early period as a civic republic through a middle period as a national republic to the liberal republic of our day. This transition is explained as an evolution from "decentralized forms of political association" to national institutions largely "insulated from democratic pressures." As a result, he concludes, we have become captured in a great paradox: the large nation state tends to "undercut the kind of community on which it nonetheless depends."

This conclusion is typical of the combination of confidence and doubt about the future of our constitutional tradition which is found in each of the essays. This generation should not escape the necessity of pondering these issues as part of the ongoing effort of free people to secure their freedom in a time of great change on both the domestic and the international levels. These six essays are put forward at this time in the hope that they will clarify some important issues and help us remember essential lessons of the past, as we continue in this great public conversation.

The four invited essays were originally presented in January of 1985 as a lecture series inaugurating the celebration of the Bicentennial of the Constitution of the United States of America at Brigham Young University. The two essays by the editors were written especially for this volume. The lecture series, the volume, and other aspects of this Bicentennial celebration were made possible by the generous support of the College of Family, Home and

Social Sciences, the College of Law, the Office of Scholarly Publications, the Department of Political Science, and the Associated Students, all of Brigham Young University.

GARY C. BRYNER
NOEL B. REYNOLDS
December 1985

Editors' Note:

As there are numerous references to, and citations of, *The Federalist* throughout this volume, for ease of location we cite consistently from Clinton Rossiter, ed., *The Federalist Papers: Alexander Hamilton, James Madison, John Jay* (New York: New American Library, 1961). At the end of each *Federalist* quotation in the text a citation is inserted in parentheses which contains the *Federalist* paper number, followed by a colon, followed by the page number where that quotation can be found in the New American Library edition. For example, quotation of the first line of *Federalist* No. 10 would be cited as (10:77).

I

CONSTITUTIONALISM AND THE POLITICS OF RIGHTS

★

Gary C. Bryner

Constitutionalism has at its roots the idea of protecting the rights of individuals and minorities from majoritarian actions. Constitutional governments are established primarily, in theory, to assure individual rights, and their constitutions are designed to assure governmental respect for those rights. The French and American revolutions of the late eighteenth century were fueled by the idea of protecting rights. For the French, the "end in view of every political association is the preservation of the natural and imprescribable rights of man."[1] For the Americans, who were more willing to prescribe at least some of the rights of man, "Governments are instituted among men" to "secure [the] rights" of "Life, Liberty and the pursuit of Happiness."[2]

The basic elements of constitutionalism are designed to secure rights. The rule of law, resting on the idea that governmental actions should be clearly expressed, known in advance, and applicable to all, permits individuals to exercise liberties assured them by right, free from arbitrary governmental interference. Constitu-

---

Gary Bryner is an Assistant Professor of Political Science at Brigham Young University.

tional structures and procedures that provide intergovernmental checks on the exercise of power can increase the likelihood that at least some political actors will seek to protect individual rights. Provisions assuring public participation in the electoral process might themselves address an important political right, as well as provide an opportunity to protect other rights. Governmental powers can be expressly provided or clearly prohibited so that areas of individual autonomy are provided and rights can be enjoyed.

Rights are attractive because they offer insulation to the exercise of individual liberties from governmental intervention. If individual liberties to vote, own property, or be free from unreasonable invasions of privacy or searches are defined as rights, then such liberties are more secure and less likely to be altered through legislative or other action than are liberties with no grounding in rights. Advocates of particular liberties have great incentives to seek the status of rights for these concerns so that calculations of economic costs or net social welfare will not be used to negate them. Ronald Dworkin's analogy is a useful one here: rights should be seen as "trumps" that are held by individuals and that can be used by them to counter majoritarian actions that seek some public purpose at the expense of the rights of individuals.[3]

Once liberties are defined as rights, they cannot be violated just because they are too expensive to provide or because the majority of the population, through their representatives, decide to spend public resources for other purposes. While rights are often thought of as individual independence from certain government actions, independence requiring only that government not take those actions, rights may actually require the expenditure of public funds. A right to a fair trial, including a right to legal counsel and psychiatric counseling, must be provided by government even if the majority would rather spend tax revenues on some other public purpose. The right to personal liberty or property might be threatened by aggression from other individuals or private organizations, thus triggering an obligation on the part of government to intervene in assuring these rights. While the majority might refuse to provide all the police protection that individuals demand, it is obligated to provide sufficient funds to secure such protection even if it is more interested in pursuing other public purposes. Proponents of welfare or subsistence rights argue that governments are obligated to assure for all citizens some minimum level of health care, education, or living standard. Once this social "safety net" is defined as a right, then it must be provided to all citizens and cannot be scaled back or abolished simply because the majority would like to spend its money on some other project or purpose.

Not all rights are understood as legal rights—rights with correlative duties that can be enforced in courts of law. Some rights are viewed by their proponents as "natural" or "moral" laws that compel respect through the force of moral reasoning or acceptance of moral norms and values. Legal rights, especially those emblazoned in a constitution, are especially valuable because of the means provided to enforce them. The duty to respect such rights falls on all whose actions might conflict with them; the duty to assure and enforce them falls on all who are part of the political society in which the rights-holders live. Individual members of the polity are obligated to take no action that violates the rights of others and are obliged to contribute to the governmental mechanism for enforcing those rights. If a polity determines that basic subsistence rights should be guaranteed to every person, then everyone has a duty to contribute to the cost of providing those rights.[4]

The exercise of an individual's rights usually infringes on the liberties of others, and often on the prerogative of the majority to take action it believes to be in the common good. Rights must be justified as appropriate limitation on the freedom of others and especially on majority activity. Rights are, for some proponents, justified by appeals to divine or natural origins; that is, they are ordained of God and must be respected, or they are inherent characteristics of humankind and are antecedent and thus superior to societal constructs and arrangements. For others, rights rest upon some fundamental moral value, such as equality, which serves as the basis for a variety of subsequent rights. Some proponents argue that rights are social constructs agreed to in order to protect individuals against the threats to them that arise in social life.

In the past, rights have generally been viewed as designed to protect individuals' interests related to choice, self-determination, and autonomy. The related duties are primarily negative, because they require that others simply refrain from obstructing action or interfering with individual choice. (There is still, of course, the positive obligation to provide the necessary resources for enforcement.) More recently, the idea of rights has, for some, evolved to include socioeconomic, welfare, or subsistence rights that include positive duties on the part of government to provide for those rights. One scholar has argued that this evolution is universally recognized: "It is not now seriously suggested that rights to liberties are the only sort of rights that can be."[5] Such a claim seems premature, at least for the American political system. Many scholars are wont to insist that rights be viewed in traditional terms of individual liberties or common law protections, or that the understanding of rights of the Framers of the U.S. Constitution be binding upon the current political generation.

All this is to make complicated what is, at its foundation, a relatively simple and widely accepted notion in liberal political thought, that individual rights cannot be sacrificed for public or common purposes. Conservative and socialist traditions that are hostile to the idea of individual rights, that reject the idea that individual claims can somehow supersede communal or societal concerns, do not enjoy much persuasive power in America, although elements of their criticism form an important part of the intellectual discourse surrounding rights (see below).

The American political system "takes rights seriously." While there is continual debate over which rights ought to be recognized, how conflicting rights should be balanced, and how some rights ought to be enforced, there is general acceptance of the importance of rights. Indeed, as some have argued, the creation of new rights and the protection of existing ones has become a growth industry, where law professors, practicing attorneys, social activists, and others aggressively push for the creation of new rights and their vigorous enforcement by government.[6] There has developed in America a "politics" of rights that seeks to employ the language and perspective of rights in making a variety of collective decisions. It seeks to expand the number and scope of rights. It seeks to employ the methodology of rights in decisions concerning the allocation of public resources.

How should we understand rights? What interests should we accept as rights? How can rights be secured? What kinds of governing devices and structures can best assure the protection of rights? What limits are there to the creation and sustaining of rights? Answers to these questions are pursued by examining how the Framers of the U.S. Constitution viewed the idea of rights and how the contemporary debate over rights addresses them.

II

The Framers were influenced by a variety of ideas. They sought guidance and direction from virtually all the sources of political thought available in the late eighteenth century. The writings of classical theorists and historians were frequently read and referred to by the Framers and others who joined in the debate over principles of government.[7] The European Enlightenment also served as an important source of ideas for political thought in eighteenth-century America. Newton and Locke, Voltaire and Montesquieu, and other reformers and philosophers were frequently cited in colonial American pamphlets in discussion of natural rights, liberty, and social and governmental contracts. Some scholars have traced the influence of Hutcheson, Hume, Smith, and other writers of the Scottish Enlightenment on the political thought of James Madison and other Framers.[8] The English common law provided an important source of the history of "human dealings embodying the principles of justice, equity, and rights."[9] The Anglo-Saxon tradition of the "inalienable natural rights of free men" was emphasized by Jefferson and others as an important source of rights for Americans.[10] Puritanism also assumed a significant place in the debate over constitutional government as it emphasized the freedom and dignity of the individual that sprung from the Puritan revolution. Finally, colonial Americans were greatly influenced by the English Commonwealthmen such as radical Whig writers John Trenchard and Thomas Gordon, who brought together strands of thought from the Enlightenment and common law, covenant theology and classical thought, and Puritan Christianity.[11]

It is, of course, difficult to understand the concepts and values of the Framers from their perspective rather than from our own prejudices, values, and preconceptions. Quentin Skinner has well summarized the dilemma:

It will never in fact be possible simply to study what any given classic writer has said . . . without bringing to bear some of one's own expectations about what he must have been saying. . . . These models and preconceptions in terms of which we unavoidably organize and adjust our perceptions and thoughts will themselves tend to act as determinants of what we think or perceive. We must classify in order to understand, and we can only classify the unfamiliar in terms of the familiar. The perpetual danger, in our attempts to enlarge our historical understanding, is thus that our expectations about what someone must be saying or doing will themselves determine that we understand the agent to be doing something which he would not—or even could not—himself have accepted as an account of what he was doing. [12]

Given these limitations, there is still value in attempting to understand how the Framers viewed important concepts such as constitutionalism and rights. Some agreement over their general understanding of rights can serve as a basis for subsequent debate and discussion.

There is at least some agreement that the Framers had in mind the following notions concerning rights. First, they were concerned with the right of self-preservation and order. Governments were to be instituted to permit individuals to secure their self-preservation. By nature, people were adversaries and a threat to one another's rights; government served to constrain all members of the polity in producing security and order. The right of self-preservation was, in part, the same as that of life and liberty. [13]

Second, the rights of individual choice, of the pursuit of happiness, and of freedom of conscience were central to the thinking of the Framers. Freedom of conscience was the underpinning of all liberty; no right was more fundamental than that of freedom of worship and belief. [14] This also included the right to acquire and keep property, since property itself could be used to pursue happiness. Ownership of property also contributed to individual independence and autonomy. "The protection of different and unequal faculties of acquiring property," Madison wrote in *Federalist* No. 10, "is the first object of government" (78).

A third right was that of self-government. The Declaration of Independence states clearly that governments derive their power from the consent of the governed, and that the people have the right to abolish their government should it fail to protect their rights. The right to form a government was extremely important, because it is government itself that guarantees all other rights.[15]

The source of these rights was usually described in terms of "laws of nature," the "nature of man," or religious belief and biblical sources. For some, rights could be deduced by understanding the nature of man: the need for self-protection, given the natural tendencies of men to encroach on the interests of one another. For others, rights found their source in God: the task of forming government was to put into human institutions laws and rights consistent with God's will. Regardless of the source of these rights, they served as the basis for the specific rights incorporated into the Constitution and its amendments.

The Framers of the Constitution appear to have had at least four means in mind for assuring the protection of rights. First, they sought to form an extended, commercial republic that would encourage the pursuit of economic activity rather than political schemes that might threaten individual rights and that would fragment interests and make their aggregation more difficult. As national boundaries were extended, a greater diversity of interests would be included in the polity. A large republic would more likely escape the class conflicts endemic in several of the states that pitted debtors against creditors, wealthy against poor.[16]

Second, the structure of government was designed to protect rights by enumerating the powers of government, by separating the functions of government, by having elected officials check each other, and by the structuring of representation. The Constitution was itself to be understood, as Hamilton argued in *Federalist* No. 84, as "A BILL OF RIGHTS"; in the preamble of the Constitution is found "a better recognition of popular rights than volumes of those aphorisms which make the principal figure in several of our State bills of rights and which would sound much better in a treatise of ethics than in a constitution of government" (513, 515). Unlike the state governments, the national government was to be one of limited powers. It could pursue only those tasks expressly given it and would thus not be a threat to individual rights.

In separating the functions of government, the Constitution avoided the concentration of power in the same officials. Madison argued that "the accumulation of all powers, legislative, execu-

tive, and judiciary, in the same hands . . . may justly be pronounced the very definition of tyranny" (47:301). There would
be, however, some sharing of power so that elected officials could
check each other. Madison explained the mechanism of checking
and balancing power in assuring that government would be restrained from encroaching upon rights: "Ambition must be made
to counteract ambition. The interest of the man must be connected with the constitutional rights of the place" (51:322). That
is, the rights or powers associated with constitutional places or
offices would be exercised by some officials as a check on the
ambition of other officials. For Madison, the most important
check was the bicameral structure of Congress. Since Congress
was the most powerful branch, the primary check on governmental excess was the need for both legislative chambers to come to an
agreement over legislative initiatives. In fragmenting power and
separating functions, the quality of decisions made promised to
improve. Rights would be more secure in a "deliberative democracy" where actions were taken only after serious debate and
discussion and review by different bodies. [17]

The structure of representation created in the Constitution
sought to protect rights in two ways. First, it extended the sphere
of government, taking in a "greater variety of parties and interests," making it "less probable that a majority of the whole will
have a common motive to invade the rights of other citizens"
(10:83). Second, as Madison argued, it would remove governing
power from the people themselves and would

> refine and enlarge the public views by passing them through the
> medium of a chosen body of citizens, whose wisdom may best
> discern the true interest of their country and whose patriotism
> and love of justice will be least likely to sacrifice it to temporary
> or partial considerations. Under such a regulation it may well
> happen that the public voice, pronounced by the representatives
> of the people, will be more consonant to the public good than if
> pronounced by the people themselves. (10:82)

Crucial to this idea of representation is that the representatives
remain uninstructed. Congress was not to be an aggregation of
interests, but was to be free from narrow interests based on land,
manufacturing, mercantile, money, and other concerns. For Madi-

son, "the regulation of these various and interfering interests forms the principal task of modern legislation" (10:79).

The third means for fostering rights is by listing them as actions in which governments cannot engage. Article I, Section 10 of the Constitution, for example, lists some actions that neither the national government nor the state governments can take, some of which directly protect individual rights. Madison, Hamilton, and others were hesitant to add a bill of rights, arguing, as indicated above, that the Constitution itself was a bill of rights. Herbert Storing has concluded that their opposition to a bill of rights came from the fear that too much discussion of rights, too much emphasis on individual, natural rights would be fatal to the development of effective government. Government needed to enjoy some presumption of legitimacy in order to be sufficiently empowered to be able to protect the liberties for which it was created. Good citizenship, a sense of community, a willingness to support government might would be threatened by too much discussion of rights. Madison eventually joined in the effort to enact a bill of rights in order to head off efforts by Antifederalists to amend the basic structure of the Constitution and weaken the fundamental powers of the national government. For Madison, the Bill of Rights sufficiently satisfied the demand to provide more directly for individual rights without compromising the Constitution itself. He eventually argued that the Bill of Rights was not particularly important, but that it was not harmful and might be of some good in protecting rights.[18]

The Bill of Rights, like most of the other amendments, reflects a concern with the basic rights discussed above. Many of the amendments seek to assure that in providing for social order and peace, rights of life, liberty, and independence are considered. Other provisions, such as freedom of speech and religion and protection from unreasonable searches, help preserve individual autonomy, independence, and freedom. Still other provisions, such as the freedom of speech, press, and assembly, and several of the other amendments, seek to structure the way self-government or elections take place.

The fourth and most important source of protection of individual rights, according to the Framers, is virtue—virtue on the part of both leaders and citizens. Madison, in his important discussion of the structure of government in *Federalist* No. 51, states that "a dependence on the people is, no doubt, the primary control on the government; but experience has taught mankind the necessity of auxiliary precautions" (322). The structure of government, the separation of powers and checks and balances, the scheme of representation—all were auxiliary to the primary protection against the inappropriate exercise of governmental power. In discussing freedom of the press, Hamilton argued "that its security, whatever fine declarations may be inserted in any constitution respecting it, must altogether depend on public opinion, and on the general spirit of the people and of the government" (84:514).

While the Federalists and Antifederalists disagreed over how to assure virtuous government, they agreed on its importance and argued together that a virtuous people were essential for republican government. Madison concluded that "no theoretical checks—no forms of government—can render us secure. To suppose that any form of government will secure liberty or happiness without any virtue in the people, is a chimerical idea."[19] Franklin warned that "only a virtuous people are capable of freedom. As nations become corrupt and vicious, they have more need of masters."[20] "Human rights," Washington wrote, can exist only "so long as there shall remain any virtue in the body of the people."[21] Government itself was necessary because of a lack of virtue, because men were not "angels," as Madison put it. The less virtue possessed by the people, the more government they need. The less able they are to exercise their rights and liberties, the greater need there will be for government coercion and limitations on individual actions.

Unlike the classical idea of virtue, where the development of virtue in the citizenry was the prime objective of government, the Framers saw virtue as a means to assure liberty and self-government.[22] In part, virtue was equated with a willingness to sacrifice individual concerns for the benefit of society as a whole. People voluntarily restrained their demands and pursuits so that liberty could flourish. Virtue was an important source of restraint and willingness to submit to the common good. Colonial Americans claimed that they possessed the qualities necessary for self-government.[23] And, in part, virtue was equated with wisdom and foresight, with enlightened leadership and statesmanship. An appeal to virtue in elected officials meant that their pride and desire for a positive reputation, as well as the pride of the people in being represented by virtuous men, would cause them to rise above selfish, narrow concerns.[24] Virtue also was associated with Christian ideals of charity and the golden rule. People were to be motivated by a sincere interest in and love for others, so that their freedom and pursuit of their own self-interest would be voluntarily constrained and limited. Society would be peaceful and harmonious without the heavy hand of government.[25]

While some of the colonial thinkers appeared to believe that virtue could be inculcated through reason, most considered its source to be in religion. The Framers were vigorously opposed to establishing a state church; their concern with freedom of conscience and religion was a fundamental right for all Americans to enjoy. They saw virtue as a product of general Christian beliefs that permeated the colonies, as well as the contribution of organized religion and family life.[26] Virtue was to be privately developed and nurtured. The state itself was not to be responsible for it; that was one of the lessons of classical politics. Since general Christianity and the different churches were already viewed as the source of virtue, government need only keep from interfering in these areas. Schools were also to play an important role in fostering virtue. The Northwest Ordinance of 1787 declared that "religion, morality, and knowledge being necessary to good government and the happiness of mankind, schools and the means of education shall forever be encouraged." Colonial schools, as Clinton Rossiter noted, were actively involved in promoting virtue, "whether designed to reinforce true religion or 'to form the Minds of the Youth to virtue.' "[27] Religious beliefs would serve as the primary source of that foundation.

III

The Framers of the U.S. Constitution, then, had a relatively limited set of rights they sought to protect. The rights with which they seemed to be most concerned related to the protection of individual liberty, independence, and freedom of thought. They did not believe that they had identified in the Constitution all rights: the Ninth Amendment states that "the enumeration in the Constitution, of certain rights, shall not be construed to deny or disparage others retained by the people." They did believe that rights could best be protected through a combination of governmental structures and procedures; listing the rights to be protected; electing virtuous leaders by a virtuous citizens, all of whom would vigilantly watch for threats to individual rights; and through the private development of moral virtues, in which a concern for individual rights would be joined with a desire to respect the rights of others and pursue the interests of the whole community.[28]

Modern proponents of rights do not all agree on the kinds of rights they seek to assure. Advocates of welfare or subsistence rights often draw upon sources such as the Universal Declaration of Human Rights, which affirms that each person has a "right to food, clothing, housing and education; rights to work, leisure, fair wages, decent working conditions, and social security; rights to physical and mental health; protection for the family and for mothers and children; a right to participate in cultural life."[29] Others who stress the obligation of government to undertake regulatory tasks also use the language of rights: "What about the rights of individuals to breathe clean air, to drink clean water, to secure drugs and food that do not have unnecessary side effects or cause illness, to have a job that does not foster concern, to drive an automobile without unnecessary exposure to death or crippling injury? These are the rights of the citizenry which regulation is designed to defend."[30] Preferential treatment for women, minorities, handicapped persons, and others is justified as a right, owed to them by society because of past discrimination. The rights of institutionalized persons, primarily prisoners and mental health patients, to better conditions of treatment have been actively pursued by federal judges. Courts have also created rights of individual privacy in areas of sexual activity and abortion.[31]

The language of rights is attractive to a broad range of arguments and concerns, as it seeks to put limits on majoritarian desires and actions in order to protect these rights. A variety of justifications for this expansion of rights has been offered, as proponents seek to create new understandings of rights. Proponents of the expansion of rights from traditional concerns of liberty and property to subsistence rights or rights of handicapped persons and other groups of individuals defend this shift in the understanding of rights as an essential response to the evolution of threats to individuals. Henry Shue, for example, argues that rights are best understood as social arrangements devised to protect members of a society. Rights are protections we grant to each other in order to shield ourselves from threats from which we cannot alone insulate ourselves. For Shue, the threat to which individuals are most susceptible is that of physical fragility. While traditional notions of rights guard against physical assaults, lack of sufficient food for an adequate diet is equally a threat to life. Individuals who are poor are likely to be children, are likely to be poor as a result of governmental or private action beyond their control, and are likely to have no opportunities to produce food themselves. Since the threat arises from social conditions, the response must also be a social one, taking the form of new rights.[32]

Other proponents of new rights find in the Constitution moral principles that serve as the basis of new rights. Owen Fiss, for example, finds in the Constitution a set of values, such as equality, liberty, due process, and property, that represent a "public morality." These values are then translated into rights grafted onto those that individuals already enjoy to assure that governmental actions affecting them are brought into conformity with this public morality. A large bureaucratic state is the primary threat to individuals' rights; now rights must be constructed in response to the evolution of the modern state in order to protect constitutional values.[33] As the state grows in size, especially in providing more and more social services to citizens, the power of bureaucrats is greatly enhanced, thus threatening the individual rights of recipients. One of the paradoxes of the welfare state is that as government expands in order to provide for certain rights it becomes more of a danger to other rights.

Some would create rights in order to give special protection to concerns and interests of particular groups that have been or are currently discriminated against. Since members of these groups are discriminated against because they are part of a group rather than because of individual characteristics, remedies take the form of group rights that can then be enforced against majority decisions.[34] Traditional civil liberties, others argue, are reinforced by the creation of new rights. Individual freedom and opportunities for self-fulfillment presuppose individual independence that comes from possessing private property. Since many individuals do not own property, state-created property, in the form of subsistence rights, can provide the kind of independent base upon which individual activity can take place. In effect, since private property is such a useful social device, it should be made widely available.[35] Traditional civil liberties are not likely to be exercised by the destitute or uneducated. Once individuals are guaranteed an adequate standard of living, they will be much more likely and able to avail themselves of their civil liberties and rights. The more available the material resources, the more effective the exertion of rights is likely to be; hence political and personal rights require at least a substantial minimum standard of living. Some have argued that the idea of civil liberties really presupposes a substantial degree of economic and social equality.[36]

For others, the problem is that economic resources can be used to alter the distribution of political rights in violation of the expectation that such rights will be distributed equally. Arthur Okun has argued that "money can buy a great many things that are not supposed to be for sale in our democracy," that economic wealth can be used to transgress almost every right. "Money buys legal services that can obtain preferred treatment before the law; it buys platforms that give extra weight to the owner's freedom of speech; it buys influence with elected officials and thus compromises the principle of one person, one vote."[37] A redistribution of income, then, serves to extend the effective existence of rights.

A politics of rights, finally, is defended as essential to moral evolution, an ongoing, vigorous evaluation of our established moral conventions. Regular legislative activity fails to address fundamental concerns; discussion of rights fosters a concern with political issues that are moral problems and facilitates moral evaluation and possible moral growth. It assumes that there are some "right" answers to political-moral problems, and that these answers can be found through the convergence of the variety of systems of moral thought that infuse political decision making.[38]

These and other arguments that have been offered in anticipation of and in defense of the expansion of rights have, of course, not gone unchallenged. Some critics argue that these new rights themselves are inappropriate. As new rights are added, the value of old ones is lessened. Rights "inflation" sacrifices the importance of traditional concerns for newer ones. One can reasonably assume that there are some limits to the expansion of rights, that the more rights there are, the less attention given to each right. But if proponents of subsistence rights can, for instance, make a convincing case that those rights are as important as traditional political rights, then there is no basis for excluding them except tradition or past practice.[39]

The swelling of rights may, in a related fashion, threaten the ability of government to accomplish the tasks required of it. The more the state intervenes to protect rights, the less of a distinction there is between public and private spheres. As social and economic outcomes are seen as the result of governmental actions, demands are stimulated. Each new intervention, like a ratchet, generates expectations for new groups to have their demands met by government. The state is eventually overwhelmed and becomes almost paralyzed; as the state is expected to perform more and more functions, it finds that it can actually perform fewer and fewer. This phenomenon is not limited to demands for new rights, but it supports the conclusion that the dynamics of rights escalation ultimately threatens the viability of government. For the state to be able to function, there must be some restraints on the demands for public action. This requires limits on the recognition of new rights.[40]

Some rights conflict with other liberties to which individuals have rights. As rights are expanded to include transfer programs funded by progressive taxes, those who pay the taxes argue that this represents a taking of their property and a diminution of their freedom. That is, of course, the nature or rights: they limit the liberties of others by imposing a duty on them. One can argue that some governmental taxation is required by the existence of rights. Since rights cannot be assured without governmental intervention, or at least a credible threat of intervention, some individual contribution is required to provide for the costs of that intervention. However, this does nothing to determine what interests should be considered rights, but only that once an interest is viewed as a right, it then imposes a duty to provide the resources for assuring that right. Nor does this resolve the problem of conflicting rights. If, for example, the protection of one's property is a right, the duty not to infringe on that right falls on all others, and all members of society are obligated to contribute to the costs of governmental mechanisms for enforcement, because without such enforcement, the right would be of no practical value and could be violated without fear of punishment. If, in contrast, the discussion is of subsistence rights, which require that the members of society all contribute from their own property, through taxes, to provide the pool of funds necessary to provide for these rights, then subsistence rights must be shown to overcome property rights.

Such an effort involves the development of a hierarchy of rights, so that choices can be made from competing rights and liberties. But what methodology do proponents of rights offer for making such judgments? One could argue that the rights recognized for the longest time, which have become part of generally accepted notions of rights, should be favored over newer rights. While even proponents of newer rights might agree that the burden of proof is on them to establish that their interest should indeed be understood and accepted as a right, they might argue that established rights should not automatically prevail. Such an arrangement is, they would likely argue, too protective of the status quo, too inflexible to respond to changes in the threats to individuals that need to be countered with rights. If there is agreement over a moral theory that can provide criteria by which these claims can be sorted out, then the prevailing right can be determined. For example, if John Rawls's principle that policies should be pursued only if they serve to make better off those who are currently worse off is accepted, then proponents of subsistence rights will likely be able to prevail in arguing that these rights should be favored since they tend to reduce inequality. If, however, Robert Nozick is the preferred source of moral principles, then the case he makes for minimal state involvement in managing the distribution of wealth points to property rights over subsistence rights.[41]

Since there is not likely to be any consensus over moral theories that can provide the basis for ranking rights, one might turn to public opinion. The appeal here would be to majoritarian sentiment: What kinds of rights does the citizenry wish to recognize and provide for? If opinion polls were to show that the public clearly supports the idea of subsistence rights and is willing to provide for them by imposing taxes and thus restrict individual liberty to control property, then such rights could be constructed and would be legitimate. But such an approach raises two objections. First, is majority sentiment the appropriate basis for defining rights? Should calculations of individual rights, understood as trumps over majority actions, be made by that majority? Proponents of judicial activism have argued that these are precisely the kinds of decisions that should be insulated from majoritarian opinions. Rights need to be considered independent of political pressures and short-run concerns.

The idea of constitutionalism, however, points in a different direction. Defining rights, placing limitations on the powers and prerogatives of the majority, is a central purpose of constitutionalism and must include the participation of the people. They alone can set these kinds of limits on the power of the majority. Popular ratification of the Constitution, the Bill of Rights, and other constitutional amendments provides the underpinning for the idea that only the people can make the kinds of choices implicit in the creation of new rights. This anticipates a different kind of objection to rights: one might be very sympathetic with the substance of subsistence rights, for example, but reject the idea that the judicial process should be the means of creating those rights. Judicial activism might be rejected as an appropriate forum for the creation of these rights because of the limitations of the process itself, the limited information available to the judges, or the nonmajoritarian nature of the judicial process.

A second difficulty is in determining the criteria by which the majority will determine specific rights. Implicit in the idea of rights is that they will be provided regardless of costs. We do not ask, when confronted with a person who has been charged with a crime for which the evidence overwhelmingly points to his guilt, whether or not society should provide a trial for him. Once a trial is determined to be a "right," then the question of whether we can afford to provide one is, by the nature of rights, no longer really at issue. If subsistence benefits are a "right," then the question of whether or not we can afford to provide for that right is not appropriate. But we cannot avoid that question. If the transfer payments required to fund subsistence rights are so great, or the recipients so numerous, that the required taxes damage economic incentives, or reduce the accumulation of investment funds or otherwise significantly dampen economic output, then we may not be able to afford those rights.

Other effects of proposed rights also raise difficulties. Some proponents of preferential treatment, for example, argue that because of past discrimination, women, blacks, and other minorities have a right to preferential treatment, implemented through a scheme of hiring and advancement quotas or some other means.

Opponents of such rights argue that the right of white males not to be discriminated against on the basis of race or sex is violated by preferential treatment. In the absence of a moral theory that we all accept and recognize that would show how to sort out these claims, we might want to examine the cost and benefits of a policy of preferential treatment. If we became convinced that the costs of such a policy clearly outweighed the benefits, then we would likely not want to pursue the effort. That is, if preferential treatment was shown to be, in effect, harmful to women and minorities by reinforcing racism or weakening the value of their accomplishments by allowing critics to claim that such accomplishments resulted from preference and not merit, one would be hard-pressed to defend that right in the face of such opposition. Why would we insist on such rights when the operation of them was harmful to their intended beneficiaries? There are few rights that we would want to guarantee if compelling evidence showed that the costs were greater than the benefits; moral philosophers might describe extraordinary examples where the disadvantages of proposed policies clearly exceeded the advantages, but such possibilities would be rare in practice.

Whatever the merits of creating rights to protect particular interests, concern over comparative costs and benefits cannot be avoided. Rights cannot be formulated and pursued in isolation; they require the commitment of resources to enforce them and a willingness of most people to comply voluntarily with them. If rights are seen as illegitimate or wrong, and most people refuse to honor them, then the enforcement costs can become enormous. Continuing the example of preferential treatment, government agencies and courts cannot monitor the millions of employment decisions made daily and must assume voluntary compliance. But voluntary compliance is most likely to spring from the perception that the preferential treatment policy or right is legitimate; it is not likely to accompany a policy widely perceived to be wrong or immoral or inconsistent with the Constitution.

The utilitarian or cost-benefit calculation is an important expectation that must be satisfied before some kinds of interests can be considered rights. One cannot ignore the possibility that the preconditions of a right may not be available, and that the right cannot be sustained. But that kind of reasoning is at odds with the idea that rights are so fundamental they should be provided irrespective of cost. If a utilitarian calculation is at the base of determination of rights, then there may be little to distinguish rights from other kinds of policies. It is difficult to see how the creation of new rights can escape utilitarian calculations, yet the idea of rights assumes something different from a comparison of costs and benefits as the basis for rights.

Finally, there is great tension between a politics of rights and a politics of community. As Michael Sandel argues, a politics of rights involves the idea of autonomous individuals, unencumbered by obligations to others, an idea that is hostile to a politics of community, which rests on the idea of shared values and common concerns. In the modern welfare state, there is conflict between the expectation of the unencumbered self and the network of obligations that citizens owe to each other.[42]

This tension between rights and community arises from at least two sources. First, the idea of rights, as a liberal idea, places primary attention on the individual. Society is a collection of independent individuals who come together in civil society, not for self-fulfillment, but for peace. They come together for protection against each other so that they can pursue their individual interests. Their objectives and concerns are all placed within an individualistic perspective. A politics of rights lends itself well to such a perspective. Rights have primarily been extended through litigation, where parties are separate and opposed to each other. The adversary system does not require any shared perspective, except that both parties agree to the process of adjudication itself and that they agree to submit to the final decision. But there is no attempt to develop a consensus or to compromise. Rather, the incentives lead toward taking extreme positions, in anticipation of a judicial decision that might "split the difference" between the parties' positions, and to concealing information which, while it might be of use to the judge in rendering a more informed decision, does not advance the party's interest and is thus not submitted.

This is not to argue against the considerable advantages of the adversary process. It is very much a marketlike process where litigants need not rely on a government official to represent their interests, but are free to make the strongest case in their behalf that they can. Government can play a relatively minor role, at relatively minor expense; the burdens of research, data collection, and analysis fall primarily upon the parties involved. But litigation does little to encourage voluntarism, cooperation, consensus building, and joint efforts. It does little to foster public spiritedness and a sense of shared responsibilities and interests. A politics of rights is highly individualistic, focusing on individual needs and concerns, and ignores common values and interests. It frames choices in terms of rejecting some claims and accepting others rather than in developing compromises and joint solutions.

One might argue that expanding rights can be a communal activity, that as we recognize and insist on common rights, we are brought closer together. Critics of the politics of rights argue to the contrary. It is divisive; it discourages the kind of voluntarism and cooperation so important in a society. It permits less governmental intervention as voluntary associations address common needs. It discourages legislatures from meeting and defining the common good and taking steps in its pursuit. It encourages individualism without encouraging the voluntarism, the restraints, and the public spiritedness requisite to life in a complex society.

IV

The questions raised in this debate are fundamental and touch at the heart of our notions of society and government. Can we consider whether the costs of providing welfare rights really outweigh the benefits, or that such rights threaten the economic health upon which all material benefits rely, without compromising the fundamental characteristics of rights? Can we pursue a two-tiered approach; that is, one "that gives an important role to consequences in the justification and interpretation of rights but which takes rights seriously as placing limits on consequentialist reasoning at the level of casuistry?"[43] Can we maintain our commitment to traditional rights and still respond to new threats that implicate new rights? What methodology can we develop to choose from competing and contradictory rights? What do these issues do to our understanding of constitutionalism? Must new rights be formally enshrined through constitutional amendment before their legitimacy can be assured? Who, if anyone, is to create new rights? Should the federal courts continue to be the focus of efforts to define rights?

Is there a middle ground? In part, we need to make distinctions and explore the consequences of different options for responding to different rights. Traditional rights are clearly threatened by a large bureaucratic state. Should we expand adjudicatory efforts to direct administrative behavior and protect individual rights? Administrative law, the system of rights of private citizens affected by administration actions, has evoked dissatisfaction and frustration. One legal scholar has argued that the "history of American administrative law is a history of failed ideas."[44] Would a more effective approach be to structure internal administrative procedures and rely more on managerial schemes and approaches mandated by law as other countries do?[45] Are rights best provided for by specifying them in statutes that instruct administrative officials, rather than relying on the general principle of due process? Different rights might be best pursued in different ways for different situations; much more attention needs to be directed toward examining how rights can best be secured.

In part, we can limit our public actions to areas where we find a convergence of ideas from a variety of perspectives and theories. Rather than seeking to find one moral system to serve as the basis of all decisions, we should look for areas where there is general consensus about what is appropriate governmental action.[46] Before declaring an interest to be a right guaranteed through governmental action, we ought to examine carefully what the costs and benefits of that action would be. If, for example, we are considering whether to declare welfare benefits as a "right," we ought to examine carefully the advantages and disadvantages, the costs and benefits of such a decision. Such an effort can consider a wide range of costs and benefits and can serve as the base for determining whether government has the ability to provide for the right. A general presumption against the creation of new rights does not signal an unwillingness to address important collective problems, but, rather, a willingness to pursue public policies on a more tentative basis, a willingness to see what works and what doesn't rather than seeking to insulate governmental activity from review and change.

In part, the determination of rights should involve the legislative branch more than it does now. Champions of judicial activism argue that members of Congress are so caught up in their efforts to gain reelection that they are concerned only in satisfying

27

interests that represent some electoral benefits, or that the courts have been more sensitive to concerns of minorities and others who are most in need of protection of their rights. A middle ground might encourage judges to continue to signal abuses of rights but limit themselves to identifying violations of rights and ordering state action without actually becoming involved in the creation of specific policies or in the details of administration. Legislatures are a more appropriate forum for making the kinds of judgments concerning the level of public resources dedicated to the provision of rights. The language of rights ought to be replaced with one of public choices, made by elected representatives.

And, in part, we ought to be more skeptical about the ability of government to pursue a constantly increasing agenda. The expectation of accountability is greatly threatened by an expanding state; the more government activity takes place, the less likely elected officials will be responsible and accountable to the people. The expansion of governmental powers should be undertaken only with great caution, with great attention to the paradox that increasing governmental powers in the pursuit of rights increases the threat to other rights. We ought to reject the idea that formal law alone can provide a sufficient basis for social life, that there is, as one federal judge has put it, "no theoretical gulf between law and morality."[47] We ought to encourage personal conduct that voluntarily respects the rights of others and is concerned with their well-being.

The state should not be viewed as the sole source of the protection of rights, but, rather, as Madison, Hamilton, and others of the Founders argued, rights depend primarily on the spirit of the people. Nor should the elaboration of laws be viewed as a reflection of the security of rights. "Law reflects but in no sense determines the moral worth of a society," writes Grant Gilmore. "The better the society, the less law there will be. . . . The worse the society, the more law there will be."[48] The less individuals are secure in their rights because of the actions of others, the more important will be government coercion in protecting those rights.

Finally, we must recognize the importance and the limits of the Constitution and the idea of constitutionalism in the protection of rights. The Constitution is a durable document, flexible and adaptive, but as it becomes politicized, its integrity is weakened. As a politics of rights seeks to manipulate the Constitution for narrow purposes, the perception grows that it is a partisan document, bogged down in debates over technicalities, rather than a framework and a process for the making of political and moral choices. Much of the debate over rights can and should be redefined as a debate over public choices and priorities, a debate that cannot be resolved by deducing moral rights from the Constitution, but can and should be pursued through the open and vigorous political discussion that the Constitution encourages.

Notes

1. Quoted in Jeremy Waldron, ed., *Theories of Rights* (New York: Oxford University Press, 1984), 1.

2. The Declaration of Independence (1776).

3. Ronald M. Dworkin, *Taking Rights Seriously* (Cambridge: Harvard University Press, 1977), chap. 7.

4. H. L. A. Hart has argued that, in one sense, rights need not be matched with a duty: "the notion of having a right and that of benefitting by the performance of a 'duty' are not identical" (Hart, "Are There Any Natural Rights?," in Waldron, *Theories of Rights,* 81). Jeremy Waldron, more generally, argues that one can define rights without specifying exactly who has the duty to provide for them. Rights should thus be viewed as requirements generated by the individual interests that are at stake. Ibid., 12–13.

5. Waldron, *Theories of Rights,* 11.

6. For a defense of such efforts, see Norman Dorsen, ed., *Our Endangered Rights* (New York: Pantheon, 1984); for a critical examination of the "rights industry" see Richard E. Morgan, *Disabling America* (New York: Basic Books, 1984).

7. See generally, Bernard Bailyn, *The Ideological Origins of the American Revolution* (Cambridge: Harvard University Press, 1967).

8. See, for example, Garry Wills, *Inventing America* (New York: Vintage, 1979); and Wills, *Explaining America* (New York: Penguin, 1981).

9. Bailyn, *Ideological Origins,* 31.

10. Isaac Kramnick, "Republican Revisionism Revisited," *American Historical Review* 87 (June 1982): 649–50.

11. Bailyn, *Ideological Origins,* 53–54.

12. Quentin Skinner, "Meaning and Understanding in the History of Ideas," *History and Theory* 8 (1969): 3.

13. See generally, Walter Berns, "Judicial Review and the Rights and Laws of Nature," *Supreme Court Review* (1983): 49–83.

14. Robert A. Rutland, "How the Constitution Protects Our Rights: A Look at the Seminal Years," in Robert A. Goldwin and William A. Schambra, eds., *How Does the Constitution Secure Rights?* (Washington, D.C.: American Enterprise Institute, 1985), 1–14.

15. Walter F. Berns, "The Constitution as Bill of Rights," in Goldwin and Schambra, *How Does the Constitution Secure Rights?,* 50–73.

16. See, for example, Gordon Wood, *The Creation of the American Republic, 1776–1787* (New York: Norton, 1969), chap. 10; Martin Diamond, *The Founding of the Democratic Republic* (Itasca, Ill.: Peacock, 1981), chap. 3.

17. See Joseph Bessette, "Deliberative Democracy: The Majority Principle in Republican Government," in Goldwin and Schambra, *How Democratic is the Constitution?*, 102–16.

18. Herbert J. Storing, "The Constitution and the Bill of Rights," in Goldwin and Schambra, *How Does the Constitution Secure Rights?*, 5–35. See also Walter Berns, "The Constitution as Bill of Rights," in that same volume, 50–73.

19. Jonathan Elliott, ed., *The Debates in the Several State Conventions on the Adoption of the Federal Constitution,* vol. 2 (Philadelphia: J. B. Lippincott, 1876), 175.

20. Albert Henry Smyth, ed., *The Writings of Benjamin Franklin,* vol. 9 (New York: Haskell House, 1970), 59.

21. Saul K. Padover, ed., *The Washington Papers* (New York: Harper, 1955), 244.

22. See Thomas Pangle, "Civic Virtue: The Founders' Conception and the Traditional Conception," in this volume, for a comparison of the classical understanding of virtue with that of the Framers.

23. See generally, Wood, *Creation of the American Republic.*

24. Wills, *Explaining America.*

25. Donald S. Lutz, "Bailyn, Wood, and Whig Political Theory," *The Political Science Reviewer* 8 (Fall 1977): 118–19.

26. See generally, Dante Germino, "Carl J. Friedrich on Constitutionalism and the 'Great Tradition' of Political Theory," in J. Roland Pennock and John M. Chapman, eds., *Constitutionalism* (New York: New York University Press, 1979), 19–31; Paul Sigmund, "Carl Friedrich's Contribution to the Theory of Constitutionalism-Comparative Government," in that same volume, 32–46.

27. Clinton Rossiter, *The Political Thought of the American Revolution* (New York: Harcourt, Brace & World, 1963), 193.

28. Nathan Tarcov argues that such a blending of concern with individual rights, the rights of others, and the fostering of civil society was at the heart of John Locke's writings and of the ideas of the Framers who drew upon his writings. See Tarcov, "A Non-Lockean Locke and the Character of Liberalism," in Douglas MacLean and Claudia Mills, eds., *Liberalism Reconsidered* (New Jersey: Rowman and Allanheld, 1983), 130–40.

29. General Assembly Resolution 2200, U.N. GAOR, vol. 21, Supp. No. 16 (1966), 418. Quoted in Michael Perry, *The Constitution, The Courts and Human Rights* (New Haven: Yale University Press, 1982), 163.

30. Joan Claybrook, "Response," *Regulation* (March-April 1981): 3–4.

31. See generally, Perry, *Constitution, The Courts and Human Rights.*

32. Henry Shue, "Subsistence Rights: Shall We Secure These Rights?" in Goldwin and Schambra, *How Does the Constitution Secure Rights?* (full citation at note 14), 74–100.

33. Owen M. Fiss, "Two Models of Adjudication," in Goldwin and Schambra, *How Does the Constitution Secure Rights?*, 36–49; Fiss, "The Forms of Justice," *Harvard Law Review* 93 (1979): 1.

34. For a discussion of this issue see generally, Owen M. Fiss, "Groups and the Equal Protection Clause," in Marshall Cohen, Thomas Nagel, and Thomas Scanlon, eds., *Equality and Preferential Treatment* (Princeton: Princeton University Press, 1977), 84–154.

35. Sylvia Law, "Economic Justice," in Dorsen, *Our Endangered Rights,* 134–59.

36. Ibid.

37. Arthur Okun, *Equality and Efficiency: The Big Tradeoff* (Washington, D.C.: Brookings Institution, 1975), 22.

38. Perry, *Constitution, The Courts and Human Rights.*

39. Shue, "Subsistence Rights."

40. See, for example, Walter Dean Burnham's discussion of this problem in Burnham, "The Constitution, Capitalism, and the Need for Rationalized Regulation," in Robert A. Goldwin and William A. Schambra, eds., *How Capitalistic is the Constitution?* (Washington, D.C.: American Enterprise Institute, 1982), 75–105.

41. See generally, John Rawls, *A Theory of Justice* (Cambridge: Harvard University Press, 1971); Robert Nozick, *Anarchy, State, and Utopia* (New York: Basic Books, 1974).

42. See Michael J. Sandel, "The Political Theory of the Procedural Republic," in this volume.

43. Thomas M. Scanlon, "Rights, Goals, and Fairness," in Waldron, *Theories of Rights,* 137–38.

44. Jerry Mashaw, *Bureaucratic Justice* (New Haven: Yale University Press, 1983).

45. In West Germany, for example, administrative law is, in effect, the law of public administration, and seeks to direct bureaucratic behavior and provide internally for the rights of individuals affected by administrative decisions. See generally, Hans Linde, "The Constitutional Supervision of the Administrative Agencies in the Federal Republic of Germany," *Southern California Law Review* 53 (1980): 601–9.

46. Perry, *Constitution, The Courts and Human Rights.*

47. J. Skelly Wright, "Professor Bickel, the Scholarly Tradition, and the Supreme Court," *Harvard Law Review* 84 (February 1971): 884.

48. Grant Gilmore, *The Ages of American Law* (New Haven: Yale University Press, 1977), 110–11.

II

THE UNCERTAIN QUEST FOR WELFARE RIGHTS

★

Richard A. Epstein

THE RISE OF TRANSFER PAYMENTS

The growth of government is an oft-told tale, and nowhere is that growth more pronounced than in the expansion of government transfers of money, goods, and services to persons in need. These transfers rest on the presupposition that all individuals have a right to personal welfare. This asserted welfare right is typically defined as the right to receive "any form of assistance—monetary payment, good, or service—provided to an individual because of his or her need."[1] The definition does not resolve in all concrete cases. It is often difficult to determine in individual cases whether a payment is a pure transfer payment, as opposed to compensation for services rendered, or a payment under a scheme of social insurance, in which the transferee has previously paid market value for the benefits received.

These questions of classification, while important, should not be allowed to conceal the historical trend. Today, transfer pay-

Richard Epstein is the James Parker Hall Professor of Law at the University of Chicago.

ments encompass a large array of programs, including aid for dependent children, food stamps, medicaid, jobs, and housing allowances, and have become a staple of American life.[2] In the short run it is possible to detect decreases in the level of government transfer payments, as some of the Reagan administration's cuts since 1981 reflect. But the long-run growth of government transfer programs of all sizes and descriptions remains one of the major developments of the post-World War II period.[3]

The Search for a Theory

Given the size of the national commitment, one might suppose that a strong and clear theory justifies the extensive system of transfer payments. But the truth is otherwise. The theoretical justification for the welfare rights behind transfer payments is still lacking. The obvious challenge to need-based transfer payments is that they are coercive actions whereby the government assumes the role of Robin Hood, taking from the rich and giving to the poor.[4] No one disputes that individuals are entitled to make voluntary charitable contributions. But it is a different matter when some people try to fund their gifts with cash taken from their neighbor's pockets. Robin Hood was a bad man with good motives. By analogy, government welfare programs are bad institutions with good motives.

To overcome this simple objection, some theory must bridge the gap between giving property to those in need and taking it from others. This task is more formidable than it sounds because the gap must be closed without imperiling the rights structure that makes it possible for individuals and society, through the labor of individuals, to generate the wealth necessary to fund the desired transfer payments. The common law rests on a long tradition that speaks of rights to individual liberty, to private property, and to freedom of contract. Common law doctrines respond powerfully to demands for personal liberty and economic productivity.

The defenders of welfare rights must decide how to respond to a simple dilemma with respect to both personal liberty and private property. On the one hand they could argue that welfare rights are paramount to common law rights. But then they must explain why welfare payments are more important than prohibitions against murder, rape, and theft. I think this solution is too extreme for anyone to accept, for reasons that go both to its practical implementation and its basic coherence. On the transferor side, how could a system of taxation ever be implemented when basic property rights and personal liberties are left wholly insecure? On the transferee side, how can providing transfer payments improve the position of their recipients if these core common law prohibitions are not respected? It would be an odd system indeed that tolerated taxation for redistribution, but that provided welfare recipients with no protection, either for the money received or for the things it purchased, against criminal depredations. Redistribution on the basis of need presupposes some respect for the prior distribution of common law rights.

Alternatively, defenders of welfare rights could admit the primacy of common law rights, and argue that the system has enough "give" to admit welfare rights. This solution seems more promising. But I hope to show that it does not yield the desired result. In the end the principles of political obligation make it difficult to reconcile traditional common law rights with welfare rights that many desire to engraft on those common law rights. This is true whether the argument relies upon deontological theories of individual rights, on consequentialist theories of social utility, or on any of their major variants and combinations.

This is not to say that claims based upon need do not have some special status. However, I think the once-common view that treated help for the needy as an "imperfect obligation"[5] uneasily captures the proper position. Caring for the poor and needy is not simply another consumption choice, on a par with the preference for chocolate over vanilla ice cream. If it were, any explanation for the substantial charitable, religious, and relief effort observed over the centuries would be incomprehensible.

The traditional common law view on entitlements reflects the distinction between legal and imperfect obligations. It treats legal obligations as enforceable by the government, but regards imperfect obligations as the subject of charity, to be enforced by an uneasy mix of private conscience and social sanction. There is no legal cause of action for the want of benevolence. The nub of the argument to support this division of labor turns on the question of costs. Common law rights can be enforced at acceptable costs while welfare rights cannot. One can assume that the moral case for making some welfare payments is compelling, yet the moral case for the legal enforcement is not, once the transaction, incentive, and political costs are identified and weighed. This essay first addresses the asymmetry between common law rights and welfare rights in order to explain why welfare rights are properly included in the class of imperfect obligations. The essay then addresses whether any standard of social welfare is in principle sufficient to account for legal protection of welfare rights, and concludes that no standard is equal to the task.

The question of welfare rights is not just a question of first principles. Thus, the final section of this essay reexamines the status of welfare rights on the assumption that we do not write on a blank slate. The inquiry is transformed into a rough mix of principles and pragmatics. We must consider what concession theory must make to take into account that government has rarely observed the limitations upon its power that a sound common law theory of obligations would suggest. The persistent pattern of deviation from proper legal principles offers the best grounds for a qualified defense of welfare rights. All too often government has been the oppressor of the poor and the needy. The problem of undoing past errors necessarily brings to the fore the "second best" issues that are always the hardest to answer. In fashioning the appropriate strategy, the danger always exists that groups insistent upon turning state power to private advantage will take over control of the government. It is therefore necessary to develop the simplest strategies for reform to limit the abuse that is so often the by-product of untrammelled discretion. On balance, no approach will provide the universal solvent. Still, I believe the best overall strategy is to attack head on the direct economic restraints upon the creation of wealth and then reduce the level of transfer payments as this process continues.

WELFARE RIGHTS: THE CASE FROM FIRST PRINCIPLES

As a general matter of political theory, the strongest defense for welfare rights would assume that they are a necessary component of any just society, and as such are entitled to equal dignity with the usual array of property, contract, and tort rights traditionally defended by the common law. A closer look at the principles of legal control, however, indicates that the case for welfare rights cannot be established on first principles alone.

Rights and Their Correlative Duties

A right is like one pole on a magnet. As the north pole must have its south pole, so any right has a correlative duty. Deciding whether to recognize welfare rights in principle requires a complete specification of all individual rights and their correlative duties. Conferring enforceable rights upon certain individuals imposes correlative duties upon others, which must be defined and enforced.

The importance of correlative duties rests not only upon the elegance of legal theory, but also upon two fixed facts of the external world: scarcity and self-interest. These two facts are intimately related, as scarcity gives birth to self-interest. In combination, the two drive evolutionary biology and through it ordinary human interaction.[6] A world without scarcity is like a game of poker with free chips: all bets are off. Any social choice becomes acceptable because it is always possible to satisfy one person without inconveniencing or incurring the wrath of another. Without scarcity, it is *always* possible to make someone better off without making someone else worse off. Who could oppose welfare rights in such a world?

Self-interest is a feature of our common humanity often ignored in analyses of welfare rights.[7] Yet only when self-interest is taken into account does the assignment of entitlements become critical and the possibility of sacrifice real. Why be egoistical if one has nothing to gain, which is the case in the absence of conflict for food, land, or affections? Ignore scarcity, and our imagination alone guides both present and future. Recognize scarcity, and the entire enterprise of normative theory becomes a responsible effort to define the permissible scope for self-interest when some claims must go unsatisfied.

Scarcity cuts across generations and cultures. Some historical writers are wary of general accounts of human nature because of the contingent and nonrepetitive nature of historical events.[8] This point is well taken when the question is how a Caesar, Napoleon, or Hitler influences the course of international affairs. But it has far less force when the question is what consequences follow when, in the day-to-day operation of a society, one set of laws and institutions are adopted in preference to another. History may be contingent in the sense that no logically necessary truths drive human behavior. But it is not contingent in the sense that no regularities govern human interactions. The comparative study of legal institutions speaks more eloquently of the similarities across cultures and ages than it does of the subtle doctrinal differences separating them.[9] The Romans' discussions of fine points of contract and tort law are understandable and relevant to the thinking of lawyers today. Neither Roman society, modern society, nor any other society could make sense of legal rules that fail to recognize crimes, torts, and contracts.

Similarly, the analysis of individual behavior and the importance of incentives based upon personal gain and loss, reputation, and affection are a constant across time. Transactions with strangers are different from those within an immediate or extended family. To ignore certain universal tendencies is to insist not on a careful historical analysis of the relevant social forces, but on a form of perpetual ad hocery that destroys understanding. One might always argue that the theoretical truths of one day are irrelevant to the next. But until the proposition is concretely demonstrated it invites armchair skepticism and not historical understanding. The arguments that follow trace out the universal implications of scarcity and self-interest, and identify certain powerful tendencies which all societies must tame to survive and flourish.

Within this framework the following proposition becomes a working first principle: No legal or political theory of rights is acceptable if it fails to generate rights and duties consistent with the limited resources that must be generated to satisfy them. As a necessary corollary, levels of production cannot be regarded as constant, independent of the scheme for distributing the goods produced. Yet this error is committed whenever the question over welfare rights is stated, "Who should get what from a stock of existing goods?"[10]

The Right to Life: What Correlative Duty?

We can now pay closer attention to the theory of welfare rights. Many of those who defend welfare rights begin by presenting a categorical right to life that suppresses the question of correlative duties. An instructive passage by McCloskey reads as follows:

> My right to life is not a right against anyone. It is *my* right and
> by virtue of it, it is normally permissible for me to sustain my
> life in the face of obstacles. It does give rise to rights against
> others *in the sense* that others have or may come to have duties to
> refrain from killing me, but it is essentially a right of mine, not
> an infinite list of claims, hypothetical and actual, against an infi-
> nite number of actual, potential, and as yet non-existent human
> beings. [11]

The above argument is the entering wedge for welfare rights.
Once a categorical right to life is stipulated, denying any person
the items needed to vindicate that right is difficult. If one has a
right to life, he has a right to be supported in time of need—a
welfare right. But from the vantage point of correlative duties and
their costs, a powerful distinction exists between the narrower
common law right to life and the broader right to life McCloskey
envisioned. At common law the correlative duties are ones of
affirmative support. The distinction between these two concepts
is critical. [12]

Envisioning a world in which each person has a duty not to kill
or maim his neighbor is easy. In principle, all persons can comply
with the commands of the law, wholly without regard to their
initial wealth or natural endowments. As each person can keep his
own, but cannot take from another, all persons and things are
governed by a unique, well-defined, and complete set of rights
and duties.

Voluntary transfers do nothing to upset the balance. Persons
only undertake obligations they think they have a fair chance of
discharging, and when they do not undertake the obligation, the
other party must bear his own loss and obtains no legal entitlements against the world at large. In this legal universe, the
government's role is to enforce these contract and property rights.
But that role is bounded, as no one is placed at risk of being
subject to affirmative obligations to some other undefined person
in the original position. Before public force can be brought to
bear against any individual, he must *act,* be it by aggression,
misrepresentation, or promise. This act requirement serves as a
filter that reduces the number of situations for which legal redress
is appropriate. The transaction costs of this world are not trivial,
but they are clearly bounded.

Conceiving of a world in which each person has in the original position an obligation to preserve or support the life of his neighbor is more difficult. At a theoretical level, individual obligations will systematically and necessarily conflict with each other. Moreover, no one can guarantee that all the obligations imposed can be simultaneously discharged from the available resources. If the burdens upon the fortunate are miscalculated, the obligations created could exceed, in the aggregate, the productive resources available to satisfy those obligations. The stability of the original position is not guaranteed as it is in the common law universe.

Furthermore, the minimum level of enforcement activity required of the legal system can be very high. No act requirement exists to serve as a threshold of individual aggression or individual promises that must be crossed before government power is invoked. The transaction costs of this system are enormous, because government must intervene before any person deviates from an appropriate course of conduct. The system then falls of its own weight, for rights and duties cannot be brought into equilibrium, theoretically or practically.

The radical disparity between these two visions of the right to life is not overcome by treating categorical rights to life as only prima facie, to be overcome in proper strong circumstances.[13] The notion of prima facie rights is congenial to the common law system in which the correlative duty to the right to life is the duty not to harm. Consent aside, persons forfeit their rights to be free of interference when they interfere with the like rights of others. Self-defense is one example.[14] The use of force justifies the victim or those who come to his aid in using force against the aggressor.

In sharp contrast, one cannot overcome the presumption generated by the broader conception of the right to life solely by looking at the aggressive conduct of its bearer. Transfer payments are not tied to past conduct. Instead, the entire debate, with or without the presumption, still can be resolved only by resorting to some undefined calculation of relative need. The ordinary *pairing up* between victim and wrongdoer so congenial to the common law[15] has not place in a world with a general right to life. Without the obvious correlative duty, there is no particular target, no single obvious neighbor, who must satisfy any particular person's needs. Of necessity, the comparative equities to resources must be more broadly based. I may be entitled to take something from somebody, but it may not be from you. Private takings are suppressed only for the violence they invite, but government takings are put in their place to benefit those not allowed to take for themselves.

Any system of welfare rights thus demands elaborate and expensive pooling arrangements for allocating resources. Yet, aggregating individuals into common pools must not be allowed to obscure the central point. Someone must still take from someone else, even if third parties mediate the transfers. The accounts must still be balanced, just as, in principle, any budget must be balanced. The shift from private lawsuit to government action obscures the linkage between rights and correlative duties, but it does not eliminate the problem correlative duties create.

All of this is not to say that a theory of negative rights is not complex. As McCloskey notes,[16] complexity is guaranteed because negative rights must run to and against all persons, both present and future. Yet, that is not an objection to the common law view. In fact, all rights against killing and maiming assume the form of negative rights. Consequently, what looks like the undisputed core of the right to life dissolves into a network of bilateral relations.

An example from legal theory explains this web of negative rights. Legal theorists often distinguish between rights in personam and rights in rem. Translated literally, this might mean that certain rights, such as contract rights, are good only against individuals while other rights, such as property rights, are good only against things. Yet the Latin shorthand should not obscure the frequently made point that, whatever their pedigree, all rights are against persons.[17] Once this is recognized, the key distinction between rights in rem and rights in personam lies in the mode of creation. Rights in rem are, as lawyers are wont to say, "good against the world" because they refer to property rights that owners acquire, by first possession or by grant from a prior owner. Rights in personam typically are against a defined person or persons with whom the owner of the property right has contracted. Only the owner, not the rest of the world, has a duty to convey the land sold. The rest of the world has only a negative duty not to obstruct the conveyance.

The complex structure of rights in rem does not, however, impose correlative duties that are expensive to enforce. Only in the infrequent case when these rights are violated does ordinary legal action ensue. The right in rem is important because it establishes a framework in which social governance is possible. In a world with large numbers of self-interested individuals, each with separate goals and ambitions, systems of property rights grow up because actual, even tacit, consent is not a foundation for social obligations. The classical common law right in rem is a way to organize human interaction by easily observable rules when voluntary contract is impossible.

THE SOCIAL CRITERIA FOR WELFARE PAYMENTS

The Benefits and Burdens of Welfare Rights

Enough has been said to indicate the powerful disparity between welfare rights and ordinary common law rights against interference by force or fraud. It is now necessary to determine whether a system of welfare rights can be engrafted upon the system of common law protections that are indispensable for any organized society.

Piercing the government veil. In a world of scarcity, all rights have correlative duties. Moreover, these duties always run against other individuals. This point may seem at first to be modest: an objection to the metaphysics of abstract entities that has brought so much of traditional philosophy into disrepute. But in practice the failure to grasp its centrality has often led political theory astray.

Writers are tempted to speak of aggregates while suppressing reference to the individuals that compose them. It is common in ordinary discussion to speak of the obligations of corporations to the public at large, their shareholders, or their customers. In the heat of political campaigns one hears that "corporations do not pay their fair share of taxes," or that "corporations are made the whipping boys for failed social programs." Yet, in each case the corporation stands for some group of individuals who have elaborate obligations to each other under a network of contracts. Therefore, to support the claim that corporations do not pay their fair share of taxes one must show, by some independent social standard that has nothing to do with corporations, that the individual shareholders who benefit from certain tax regimes escape their fair share of taxes, directly or indirectly.

The same linguistic clarity is required in speaking about the public at large or the government. It is a convenient, but misleading, shorthand to say that government funds welfare rights. What is necessarily meant is that certain individuals, invested with state power, tax from some and pay to others. Saying that funding welfare rights does not fall on individuals violates the scarcity assumption. A system of welfare payments without taxation is the social equivalent of a perpetual motion machine.

Yet, to speak of taxes only scratches the surface of the problem. Most individuals are simultaneously benefited and burdened by welfare programs. They must contribute to programs from which they are, in principle, eligible for benefits. As everyone is on both sides of the transaction, it is tempting to say that legal rights and duties related to welfare programs are a giant wash. Empirically, this claim is very odd because, if true, it renders unintelligible any political defense of or attack on welfare programs. The claim is also incorrect analytically. People are not indifferent to transfer programs because the rights and duties they create are *not of equal value* to all participants. Some gain more than they lose, and others lose more than they gain. Gainers will tend to support the program, and losers will tend to oppose it.

Two reasons explain why benefits and burdens are not of equal value. First, all individuals do not bear the same percentage of the obligation that they bear of the right. As a result, when rights and duties are netted out, each person may have some residual benefit or burden. Ninety percent of a $1,000 burden is not offset by 10 percent of the parallel benefit, and the net $800 ($900 minus $100) transfer exceeds the outright confiscation and transfer of a $500 item. The ability of these non-pro rata transactions to implicitly redistribute wealth lies at the heart of concern with the law of both corporations and government. Implicit redistribution bears heavily on the theory of welfare rights.[18]

Second, the benefits conferred may take the same form as the costs imposed. Cash may be taken and in-kind benefits may be returned. In-kind benefits have different values to parties who receive them under a uniform scheme. Parties who value the benefits in excess of the cost will be net winners. Parties who do not will be net losers. The net transfer may be disguised, because everyone is both a transferee and a transferor, but viewed as a comprehensive plan, the net shifts are real. The social security system has a formal equality of benefits and burdens, but net benefits, which depend heavily upon age, introduce a massive wealth transfer from the younger to the older generation.

Two further elements must be introduced to make sense of transfer programs. The first is the idea of the baseline or original position. The second is the tripartite distinction among positive sum games, negative sum games, and zero sum games.

The baseline for fair exchange. In order to determine who wins, who loses—and by what amount—through government action, the point of departure for the process must be known. Finding the first yardstick lies behind the account that Locke, for example, gives to natural rights of person and property. Without knowing the baseline it is very difficult to determine how much compensation, if any, is owed when new rights are created and old ones are destroyed or limited. Without knowing what people have as of right, determining what they have gained or lost through government action is impossible.

Within the common law system, two premises dominate: the belief in self-ownership and the proposition that ownership in external things is acquired by first possession. Together, these premises establish a uniform baseline from which subsequent calculations can be made. One problem with this theory is that even though there is a gap between "is" and "ought," no natural necessity requires an assignment of rights to close that gap. This objection is, in one sense, so strong that it precludes all normative argument about rights,[19] including welfare rights. The point here is critical. If one could argue, for example, that all mankind owned the fruits of the earth in common, then redistributive taxation would lose much of its sting. The system of taxation would no longer be designed to take from some in order to give to others. Instead it would only *return* to people at large those things they owned in the first instance. To take a line from Finnis: "For in establishing a scheme of redistributive taxation, etc., the State need be doing no more than crystallize and enforce duties that the property-holder *already* had."[20]

Yet, here the argument depends critically on two assumptions. First, some or all original entitlements were held in common by, or at least for the benefit of, all present and future generations. Second, taxation in fact only returns to the common pool compensation to the public for what individuals have taken from it. Once it is conceded that no necessary truth exists in the common law rules of self-ownership and first possession, then the inquiry turns from the past to the future. The important question becomes what system of rights will promote the welfare of all individuals present and future?

On this score one clear utilitarian weakness of collective ownership is that it creates serious problems for the managing of resources. If individual talents are still individually owned, then claims of redistribution only run to the value of natural resources, whose value in their original condition is very small compared to the privately owned labor used to develop them. The pool available for redistribution, even redistribution to people in need, is small. On the other hand, if talents are not individually owned, but are held in some kind of Rawlsian common pool, then the scope for permissible redistribution becomes much greater because all resources are necessarily collectively owned.[21]

Nonetheless, any system that places either natural things or human talents in the common pool has serious utilitarian disadvantages. The collective ownership structure necessarily created by such a system makes determining who has control over the rights in question very difficult. If some collectivity can control common goods by taxation, then it can regulate the use and disposition of those goods as well by whatever devices it has at its command. Since no single person has clear title to any particular resource, individual efforts to sell property necessarily will be thwarted. The net effect is that any effort to equalize endowments of overall talents will materially shrink the overall level of wealth and satisfaction those talents can create.

In sharp contrast, the common law private property system has powerful utilitarian virtues. The common law system sets the stage for positive sum transactions by endowing all individuals with a set of well-defined rights that can then be exploited by use or by transfer to others.[22] The rule of first possession thereby benefits those people who are *not* able to obtain natural resources out of their unowned condition. In addition to their own labor, they have enhanced opportunities for exchange to offset the losses created by failure to obtain original acquisition. The question is whether the value of these opportunities for contracting equals or exceeds the value of the right to claim natural resources, which have all been taken by others. To some extent the answer is speculative, but it seems highly likely that the gains to the later generation exceed their costs. A system of well-defined private rights increases the resource base, which redounds to the benefit of latecomers as well as early risers. Emigrants often abandon property in corrupt societies to pay for the opportunity to work in freer societies. They make the judgment, with their feet, that a system of private rights benefits latecomers by offering enhanced opportunities to dispose of labor.

Positive, negative, and zero sum games. How can a system of welfare rights be engrafted onto this common law structure? In part it is done by arguing that it is permissible for rights to conflict.[23] But once contradiction is admitted into the system, how is it to be resolved? At this point the defense of welfare rights depends upon some more powerful theory that coordinates the two sets of rights.

One convenient way to analyze departure from the common law baseline is to resort to game theory and social choice models. A "game" is a set of moves, defined by rules, that each player makes with a set of endowments from a given initial condition. It could be the moves in a game of chess or it could be the prices at which goods or services are offered for sale in the market.[24] A positive sum game is one in which the total utility, or wealth, of the separate players is increased when the game runs its course. A negative sum game is one in which the total utility, or wealth, of the separate players is decreased. A zero sum game is one in which the total utility, or wealth, is constant, even if the size of some or all players' shares change. The distinction between these three types of games is critical for understanding the theory of rights. In principle, it suggests that only those collective moves that result in positive sum games should be allowed to vary baseline common law rights. The most obvious illustration of a collective move that should be allowed is government taxation or regulation to provide collective goods that market action could not generate because of transactional difficulties. Forming government to control internal, and combat external, aggression best illustrates a positive sum game.[25]

The analogies can go further. They can cover public roads and a system of courts. Since all persons benefit from these institutions, taxation that requires all persons to pay their pro rata share is wholly appropriate. This is true even if, as the endless battles over government contracts show, enormous care must be taken to control corruption. Other government initiatives, such as some restrictions on monopoly behavior, are also plausible under this view, given the economic models that point to the real possibility of social loss from voluntary contractual restrictions upon competitive behavior.

If welfare rights are not meant to displace the rules that govern theft, murder, and contract generally, then the strongest argument for their social creation is that they generate positive overall utility or wealth, which rich and poor alike can share. The absolute nature of the original common law entitlements is replaced by a rule that says that the rights so created may be removed, but only if rights of equal or greater value are given in their place.

Arguments that welfare rights fall into this mold are often made. They are attractive because they blunt the charge of theft, not by asserting that welfare restores rights to some original common ownership, but by assuring compensation is paid to the putative victims of the government programs. In effect, the argument is that welfare rights are acceptable because they are Pareto superior, leaving all parties better off than they would be in a world in which welfare rights are banished.[26] Nonetheless, such arguments fail on economic grounds, as will be shown later.

Welfare Rights as a Negative Sum Game

Wellman, in his book on welfare rights, offers a defense that takes this form. In defending Aid to Families with Dependent Children (AFDC), Wellman argues that it is a positive sum game in which all players end up with some share of the social gain.

> No elaborate argument is needed to show that it is much much better for these individuals to have nourishing food rather than nothing or very little to eat, decent housing rather than unheated and unsanitary shelter, if any, etc. The primary utilitarian case for making it a duty to pay AFDC is the tremendous good achieved for the recipients by the payments of the welfare agency . . . .

47

In addition to the direct benefits for the individual recipients, a program of acts paying AFDC probably indirectly benefits our society as a whole by helping to solve some of our most serious social problems.

. . . Giving aid to dependent children will help solve the problem of underconsumption. Our society is prone to economic stagnation, recession, and even depression because goods and services we produce are not purchased in sufficient quantities. Although dependent children desperately need many of these goods and services, their need cannot be translated into economic demand unless they have some source of income. Financial aid to dependent children is an efficient way of putting purchasing power where it will be used to stimulate our economy, maintain production, and reduce unemployment.[27]

Wellman also makes parallel arguments for undereducation and ill-health.[28]

The central point of the argument is that welfare rights under the AFDC program are, at least for groups, Pareto superior to a pure common law world. Stated otherwise, both payors and recipients of AFDC benefits are better off by the operation of the program, even if transferees get a larger fraction of the gain than transferors. At the very least the argument is overgeneral. It may explain why the optimal level of welfare payments is not zero, but it does not provide any reason why there should be an upper bound on transfer payments, or how that bound might be determined. If one billion dollars in transfer payments feeds the hungry and stimulates the economy, then two billion should be even more beneficial. In the extreme, therefore, why not devote the entire budget to welfare expenditures?

An endless expansion of welfare rights is only a dream because other factors, not mentioned by Wellman, account for the nonlinear relationship between overall social welfare and transfer payments. Wellman has demonstrated only that recipients of benefits are better off than they were before. However, to justify welfare payments as Pareto improvements, one must show a connection between the payments and aggregate levels of social welfare. To show that connection, one must demonstrate that the *payors'* indirect benefits exceed their direct costs.

The argument becomes more tenuous when we look at the asserted relationship between underconsumption and social ills.

By definition, any welfare benefit is a transfer payment. The benefit may increase the purchasing power of the persons who receive it, but this gain is offset by a loss in the purchasing power of the persons taxed to fund the transfer payments. Simple transfer payments do not increase or decrease consumption. If under-consumption is a problem without welfare rights, then it remains a problem with welfare rights.

Wellman's basic point might be saved by noting that the poor have a greater tendency to consume at the margin than the rich. But the welfare implications of the point remain problematic because increased consumption is purchased at the expense of reduced overall levels of saving and investment. This reduction in turn reduces levels of production and consumption in the next generation, with its own welfare recipients. The empirical tradeoff between investment and consumption does not change the basic point: *ex nihilo nihil.* No system of transfer payments can increase the amount of basic resources.

Thus far the criticisms of Wellman treat welfare payments as a zero sum game. I have assumed benefits to recipients are balanced by costs to payors. However, this conclusion is overoptimistic. At least as to wealth, transfer payments more likely create a negative sum game.

First, administrative costs of the welfare system do not benefit recipients. Taxes must be collected and benefits must be paid out. Both of these undertakings are very expensive. Any resort to a system of progressive taxation implies higher marginal tax rates. Higher marginal tax rates create stronger incentives to conceal income from taxing authorities. Government officials must then take more powerful countermeasures. Furthermore, any system of transfer payments requires some determination of eligibility and benefit levels. The net worth of current recipients must somehow be assessed to operate the program, even under a negative income tax program. These problems could be minimized by a well-run government operation and by clear statutes. However, government operations are seldom efficient and statutes are almost never clear. Even if government were efficient and statutes clear, the costs of transfer programs would not be reduced to, or even close to, zero.

Second, social and political processes used to establish and administer these benefit programs produce some side effects. The point is a familiar application of the general theory of rent-seeking behavior.[29] An economic rent is a surplus payment above "the amount that a factor must earn in its present use to prevent it from transferring to another use."[30] A person who earns $1,000 per day as an athlete may only have an income of $100 as a laborer. The $900 represents the rents accrued from the difference between working as an athlete and working as a laborer. Rent seeking involves effort to tax away some portion of that gain, in the hope that the tax will not alter the original pattern of production of the party taxed. Nonetheless, the process always generates resource losses. The effort to obtain funds for transfer payments consumes resources to protect the rents and stimulates the owner of the asset to expend real resources he now enjoys. No matter who wins the struggle, resources are diverted from the production to the transfer of wealth. This is a negative sum game.

Transfer payments to those in need are not immune from the rent-seeking dynamic. Wellman notes that it is possible to enact a system of welfare rights definite in form and specific in content.[31] True enough, but how are these statutory figures established? Within the political process, expected net taxpayers, as a group, will spend real resources to oppose welfare programs; expected net recipients will spend real resources to support them. No matter which side wins, the expenses on both sides come out of the social pie. As the theory of rent seeking predicts, the political game has a distinctly negative character.

Finally, social losses arise even after the system is in place because individual actors respond, in their production and consumption, to the incentives the welfare system creates.[32] At the extreme, high welfare benefits will induce large numbers of individuals to forego gainful activities because they are better off receiving welfare benefits.[33] Lower welfare benefits will have similar effects, but of smaller magnitude. Humane efforts to raise benefit levels, therefore, face a dilemma. In an effort to improve the lot of the very needy who now receive benefits, others are induced to enter the system, even at the cost of earning less by their own endeavors. If benefits are increased, the expected number of persons receiving benefits will increase because there is no way to keep marginal wage earners out of the welfare system once benefits are raised.

The consequences extend from patterns of consumption to patterns of production. The departure of able persons from the labor markets to the welfare markets reduces the tax base of the nation and thereby increases the tax burden on those left in the market. Accordingly, tax rates have to rise to meet the new demands, which in turn makes marginal producers into marginal recipients, thereby initiating another round in the cycle. One great problem in running a welfare program, therefore, is finding the stable stopping place, a problem ignored by Wellman and those who make similar arguments.

In this regard, the old categorical programs, which provided benefits for the blind and those in similar situations, had a certain commendable rigidity. It was highly unlikely that anyone would court blindness to obtain welfare benefits. The newer rules have precisely the opposite effect. The loose eligibility standards based on need create a substantial moral hazard that potential recipients will reduce production, a social cost, to obtain direct payments, a private gain. In short, the political dynamics of welfare payments make it difficult to confine them to a relatively limited role, even if such were ideal. Some limited measure of welfare support may meet the strict requirements of a sound social welfare program. But a government-sponsored program, once introduced, likely will grow beyond those narrow limits.[34]

Utility and Risk Aversion: An Escape from the Negative Sum Game?

A claim of either Pareto optimality or simple wealth maximization likely cannot support a welfare system, when measured at the time the system is introduced. It may, however, be possible to save the system of welfare rights for two reasons. The first speaks of the difference between utility and wealth.[35] The second addresses risk aversion at the time when choices about welfare rights are made.

On the first point, it could well be that while total wealth is diminished, utility gains to the poor may exceed utility losses to the rich. If this were the case, the welfare system could be saved. The theory is that gains to the truly needy, measured by the utility of avoiding starvation or worse, are so great they offset the losses suffered by others.

The first point can be fortified by relying upon the second: under the universal (or, at least, frequent) level of risk aversion, individuals are willing to pay real income to avoid future uncertainty.[36] A system with a welfare component compresses the distribution of incomes that emerges over time. Thus, while transfer payments may reduce total wealth, the utility of that wealth may increase. This would leave a net benefit to society, even if all members of society do not share equally the gain from transfer payments. The utility gains to recipients exceed the utility losses to payors, even as the wealth losses to payors exceed the wealth gains to recipients.

If one started behind the veil of ignorance, or, in other words, in a world in which persons knew of the general rules of human and social interaction, but not of their own position in that world,[37] then one would not know whether he would be a winner or a loser in the welfare payment system. Accordingly, a system with welfare payments might have some presumptive attraction. The person behind the veil would be willing to surrender some measure of his liberty to obtain greater personal security.

However, this veil condition is not often satisfied, given that political lines are usually well drawn when welfare programs are before the legislature; in real settings, most people know whether they will gain or lose. However, even if people were ignorant of who will gain and who will lose, the consequences are not clear. The risk aversion argument would be decisive if wealth levels could be held constant once welfare rights were introduced. But they cannot.

As a result, the case for a system of welfare rights depends upon the relative magnitude of different factors. How intense is the preference to avoid risk? Some individuals may prefer a fixed payment of forty cents to an even chance of getting a dollar. Others may require only twenty-five cents. Clearly, if individuals require only twenty-five cents, there would be more reason to support a welfare system than if individuals require forty cents. Yet, it becomes progressively more difficult to make any sense of the situation if the levels of risk aversion are not constant across the population. Levels of risk aversion are, of course, not constant for the same reason that human height is not constant. All distributions have positive variances. Thus, even behind the veil of ignorance, we face a problem: Do we follow the lead of the most cautious, the least cautious, the median person?

Furthermore, one needs to compare the gains from risk aversion to the administrative and allocative losses that are introduced. If the loss in wealth is large enough, even the poorest in society may be worse off than they would have been in a system in which they received no benefits at all. Again, the empirical evidence is not conclusive, but some of it is quite disturbing. It suggests that the large increases in transfer payments over the past thirty or so years have produced little if any benefit to society.[38] Comparisons are difficult when these disquieting points are raised. For some very risk-averse persons, the gains in security will outweigh the losses in wealth. For less risk-averse persons, losses in wealth will outweigh the gains in security. For any risk-preferring persons the social institutions have a double whammy effect: a smaller share of a smaller pie. Thus, while risk aversion drives the case for welfare rights, it is only one determinant of overall utility. It is not strong enough to dominate the other factors that influence production.

Finally, private organizations can discharge welfare functions. The family is, in effect, a system of coinsurance in which the more able members take care of their less fortunate relatives. Friendly societies and religious groups have somewhat weaker bonds but work from a broader base. Yet the strength of families and voluntary associations is eroded if it is commonly known that tax revenues are available to pick up the slack. It would be an irresponsible generalization to assume that mutual assistance within families and voluntary associations ceases once welfare rights are established. That has not happened, nor should it happen as long as families and voluntary associations can more efficiently provide support. But even if these alternative institutions are not destroyed, their role is unmistakably weakened by welfare benefits. The greater the welfare benefits, the lower the reliance upon other forms of assistance. To some extent, therefore, transfer payments made through the political process are undone by a reduction of those made outside of it. The same can be said of charitable transfers for the benefit of the poor and the needy.[39]

In short, as a matter of principle, the case for welfare rights suffers from at least two difficulties. First, there is the question of how they can be reconciled, if at all, with the system of common law rights that no one wishes to displace in its entirety. Second, if that displacement is to come it must rest upon some measure of social welfare. Any Pareto optimal claim will fail because the transfer payments will tend to leave the parties who are compelled to make transfers under the tax laws worse off than they were before. Any simple wealth maximization claim is doubtful because the wealth gains to the poor will most likely be smaller than the losses to the rich. Finally, any test of aggregate social utility is, at best, problematic even if interpersonal comparisons of utility can be made. It is necessary to balance heavy imponderables to determine whether the security, if any, obtained by forced transfers exceeds the associated costs, both administrative and productive, required to obtain that security.

Even if all these burdens are overcome, the payoff for a theory of welfare rights is quite low. At best, the proof generates only an existence theorem that states under some circumstances that some welfare rights may be justified by one criterion of social welfare. It does nothing, however, to justify the vast proliferation of programs of cash and in-kind transfer payments presently in place. No categorical or *a priori* reason blocks this inquiry, or rules out the possibility of a second tier of welfare rights in an otherwise common law world. However, economic theory does suggest that the odds are not promising for making a case for welfare rights on first principles.

SOCIAL IMPERFECTIONS AS A SOURCE OF WELFARE RIGHTS

The arguments from first principles all assume that the world has been well organized from its inception and that the only question is whether the system of welfare rights fits into this harmonious scheme. The assumption that social arrangements are well ordered is, however, false. Even in the best of times, the world of practical politics is very untidy. Legislatures and courts have grown weary and suspicious of the simple entitlements to liberty and property and have routinely created welfare and other rights. The statute books brim with legislation limiting the power of individuals to enter into contracts to dispose of their capital or labor. The need to protect the incompetent from their own foolishness may justify some of these statutes, but far too often the statutes are a response to very powerful interest groups that understand all too well how to reap supracompetitive profits by erecting legal barriers against their rivals. In some instances the rich erect these barriers against the rich, as with the restrictions imposed upon the business transactions of banks and insurance companies, or with various forms of regulation of transportation, trucks, and airlines. In other cases, however, the restrictions are directed against the poor, as with minimum wage legislation and many of the modern mandatory collective bargaining programs.

In essence, the argument here adopts and refines a theory of "social causation" to the case for welfare rights. The gist of the argument is that since individuals in need often have need through no fault of their own, the fault lies with society at large. Children who need food and sick persons who need medical attention are often not to blame for their condition, and hence society is responsible. As a general argument, the theory fails to take into account the tight restrictions on a theory of causation. The victim's blamelessness does not mean that society is at fault. Some insolvent third party—for example, a neglectful or addicted parent or an unchecked aggressor—could be responsible. Or maybe no one is responsible for the loss, if, for example, it comes from a birth defect or lightning. In any event, simple proof that an innocent plaintiff has a need never establishes that a given defendant is responsible. Lack of contributory negligence does not state a good cause of action.

If personal losses are attributable to third parties or natural events, it follows that the party who suffered the loss has no claim on the government. No causal linkage exists between one individual's harm and the conduct of other persons who must answer for that harm through taxation. Nonetheless, once legal and institutional barriers to trade are taken into account, the theory of causal intervention gains force. The government, or those who control its apparatus, has conspired to interfere with the prospective advantage of others by the use of public force. The private wrong of interfering with prospective advantage is an old one, but even so it supplies a theory of causation that works in both the private and the public sphere.[40]

This is not the place for an extended critique of various programs of public regulation and the specific harms they work on the parties they restrain. For our purposes the central point is this: *The more entrenched a network of restrictive practices against the poor, the stronger the case for welfare rights to protect them from victimization.* The problem is now one of "second best." If welfare rights have, at best, a precarious status in a perfect world, it does not follow that they have no place in an imperfect world. When political forces make eliminating legal barriers to gainful labor impossible, compensating those deprived of, or limited in, the opportunity to earn their daily bread becomes credible.

In principle, one could say to the poor youth who wants to work: "We believe that there is no sound case for welfare rights, but as a people we can do nothing to repeal the minimum wage laws—to take but one example—even though they increase unemployment. Therefore you must bear the brunt of these laws, because one deviation from principle can never justify another. Two wrongs do not make a right."

Yet this argument cannot be accepted in this naked form. In a perfect world, the relationship between two wrongs never arises because the first is always instantly corrected. But in a world of friction and intrigue, introducing a second wrong may be a proper, if risky, alternative given that the original wrong remains unredressed. Ideally, it would be burdened with neither, but if the second wrong tends to offset the first wrong, then we may be better off with both together. The statute books may list welfare rights under one head and labor regulations under another. Law schools may teach them separately. But as a matter of political theory the two areas are inextricably connected.

One powerful justification for taking a hard line against welfare rights is that persons are already endowed with a set of common law rights that allow them to fend for themselves. Though those common law rights are abridged by collective social action, no compensation is provided for those victimized by the social action. Yet, once some form of collective action upsets the original balance, maintaining the hard line that precludes all other forms of collective action is unattractive. This is true even though an inescapably bad fit exists between the wrong and the remedy. Although a system of economic restrictions may be supported only by some, a system of taxation usually imposes the costs of welfare rights upon all, even those who had no role in passing the restrictive legislation. Schematically understood, the system of welfare rights makes A pay in part for wrongs of B in order to ensure that C is compensated for the losses inflicted by improper economic restrictions to which A is hostile or indifferent. But overpayment by A may be the only way to ensure part payment by B, so the tradeoff between them is as uneasy as any we might be called upon to make.

It does not follow, however, that no rough guidelines exist for action. The first course of action is to repeal the restrictions on capital and labor to weaken the case, and the need, for welfare benefits. Yet, even if the restrictive laws, such as the minimum wage law, were repealed tomorrow, their effects would linger. Any restrictive law powerfully influences the willingness and ability of parties to acquire skills or a trade. Repealing the law does not instantly correct the reduction in the formation of human capital that stems from past enforcement of that law. The bad effects will survive the law's demise. Simple repeal of past legislation does not return us to the same economic and social position that would have existed had the legislation never been passed.

Thus, the proper program for welfare rights is an unhappy combination of high principle and muddling through. We should undo restrictions on production, moderate the size and scope of the welfare obligation, and recognize the imperfect congruence between the remedies proposed and the wrongs redressed. Given our heritage of legislative error, it seems foolish to assert that the cleansing of the social order should begin with the welfare system now in place. Once the minimum wage, to revert to my stock example, is gone, the relative attraction of working, say for teenagers, will increase and the attractiveness of welfare systems will decrease—even if benefit levels remain constant. As the number of persons dependent upon welfare is reduced, the tax burdens should fall as well. Furthermore, the process can be hastened as many restrictions on capital and labor wear out over time. For example, inflation repeals by degrees a minimum wage for a fixed dollar amount. As the restrictions are relaxed and more individuals rejoin the labor force, the welfare problem becomes more manageable.

However, at present I think it is fair to say that this approach of relaxing restrictions on capital and labor could not garner the necessary support from the political process. But the questions are capable of reasoned argument, and reasoned argument might influence, in some way, the future course of collective action. There is, rightly, an enormous diffusion of power in any democratic society, so that any program of change will meet with strong resistance. Yet, even small changes on so important an issue can have dramatic social consequences.

CONCLUSION

We are now in a position to assess why welfare rights have always proved vexing and troublesome. The combination of the ideal and the real explains why the foundations of welfare rights are neither necessarily secure nor necessarily unsound. The purist arguments that tug against recognizing welfare rights are always at war with the historical and time-bound arguments for creating, or at least preserving, welfare rights. The quest for welfare rights is therefore uncertain, and for good and sufficient reason will remain so.

Notes

1. See Carl Wellman, *Welfare Rights* (Totowa, N.J.: Rowman and Littlefield, 1982), 30.

2. One marginal case is social security. When combined with a regressive tax structure, social security has both insurance and welfare components. As a result, including social security in this list of need-based benefits would be controversial, and for the purposes of the more general argument it is not critical whether it is included. This essay focuses on the justification for welfare rights, not on the classification of different programs. In general, when I speak of transfer payments I mean those that are geared to need, and thus, for convenience, I exclude other types of transfer payments, such as crop subsidies, which are purportedly justified on other grounds, which I think are wholly insufficient in principle.

3. For some indication of the growth in these programs, see Charles Murray, *Losing Ground* (New York: Basic Books, 1984), 14:

> The period we will cover, 1950 to 1980, saw extraordinary changes in the nature of those transfers. Consider just the money, on just the core programs—federal social welfare expenditures in 1950 alongside 1980, using a constant, official definition and constant dollars as the basis for the comparison:
> • Health and medical costs in 1980 were 6 times their 1950 costs.
> • Public assistance costs in 1980 were 13 times their 1950 costs.
> • Education costs in 1980 were 24 times their 1950 costs.
> • Social insurance costs in 1980 were 27 times their 1950 costs.
> • Housing costs in 1980 were 129 times their 1950 costs.
>   Overall, civilian social welfare costs increased by twenty times from 1950 to 1980, in constant dollars. During the same period, the United States population increased by half.

A similar tale is told in James Gwartney and Thomas McCaleb, "Have Antipoverty Programs Increased Poverty?" *The Cato Journal* 5 (1985): 1. One key point is that the percentage of the population below the poverty level decreased sharply in the years before the modern expansion of welfare programs began in 1965, and only slightly thereafter. Ibid., 1–2.

Another recent measure of the growth of transfer payments suggests that the level of transfer payments as a percentage of personal income in the United States has increased from 3 percent to 14 percent over the past 30 years. Joseph A. Pechman and Mark J. Mazur, "The Rich, the Poor, and the Taxes They Pay: An Update," *Public Interest* 77 (1984): 28–29.

4. See Stephan Chapman, "The Bishops and the Economy," *Chicago Tribune,* 15 Nov. 1984, sec. 1, 22, col. 4. Chapman says:

> But the bishops are not satisfied with trying to stimulate greater charity by their parishioners. They also insist that the government forcibly redistribute income from the affluent to the poor: "Society has a moral obligation . . . to ensure that no one among us is hungry, homeless, unemployed or otherwise denied what is necessary to live with dignity." They tolerate no dissent: "There can be *no legitimate disagreement* on the basic moral objective" (emphasis added) [from a bishop's pastoral letter].
>
> Apparently they confuse Jesus Christ with Robin Hood. In his most dramatic statement of the Christian's charitable obligations, Jesus tells a rich young man to "sell what you possess and give to the poor" (Matthew 19:21). The bishops would tell the young man not only to sell what he has, but also to confiscate his neighbor's property and give it to the poor.

5. The view, for example, was held by Joseph Story. See, e.g., his "Natural Law," in *Encyclopedia Americana,* ed. F. Lieber (1836), reprinted in James McClellan, *Joseph Story and the American Constitution* (Norman: University of Oklahoma Press, 1971), 313.

6. For the connection, see, e.g., Jack Hirschleifer, "Economics from a Biological Viewpoint," *Journal of Law and Economics* 20 (1977): 1.

7. See, e.g., Wellman, *Welfare Rights,* and Rodney Peffer, "A Defense of Rights to Well-Being," *Philosophy and Public Affairs* 8 (1978): 65, where the point is not even mentioned when extensive claims for welfare rights are made. Political and moral philosophy flounders without some descriptive theory about how individuals will behave in response to the incentive structures that legal rights create. "Ought implies can" is an old statement of moral philosophy that must be remembered in this context.

8. For an example of such thinking in the legal setting, see Robert Gordon, "Historicism in Legal Scholarship," *Yale Legal Journal* 90 (1981): 1017. For my antihistoricist views about legal doctrine in general, see "The Static Conception of the Common Law," *Journal of Legal Studies* 9 (1980): 253.

9. With reference to the Roman Law, I have discussed some of these points at length in "The Static Conception of the Common Law."

10. See, e.g., Rodney Peffer, "A Defense of Rights to Well-Being," 69, relying upon H. J. McCloskey, "Rights," *Philosophical Quarterly* 15 (1965): 115. The error is also apparent in the position of the bishops, attacked by Chapman, "Bishops and the Economy."

11. McCloskey, "Rights," 118.

12. It is critical in speaking about other areas as well. Freedom of speech is a constitutional virtue, but the correlative duty is noninterference by government. The freedom does not confer the right to a subsidy from government funds, raised by taxes on others who may disagree with the message of the speech so subsidized.

13. See, e.g., Peffer, "A Defense of Rights to Well-Being," 75–76.

14. I have talked about the limitations on self-defense in "Intentional Harms," *Journal of Legal Studies* 4 (1975): 391, 410–20.

15. Indeed, much of my own writing on the law of torts uses the system of presumptions to give successive approximation to the proper legal position of the parties in a common law universe. See "A Theory of Strict Liability," *Journal of Legal Studies* 2 (1973): 151; "Defenses and Subsequent Pleas in a System of Strict Liability," *Journal of Legal Studies* 3 (1974): 165; "Pleadings and Presumptions," *University of Chicago Law Review* 40 (1973): 556.

16. See McCloskey, "Rights."

17. See Wesley N. Hohfeld, *Fundamental Legal Conceptions as Applied in Judicial Reasoning* (New Haven: Yale University Press, 1919), 67–75, for his discussion of "paucital" and "multital" relations, designed to capture the distinction between rights in personam and rights in rem. The weakness in Hohfeld's argument is that he did not understand the substantive reasons why a complete legal system must have rights of both property and contract that are created in very different ways.

18. For an exhaustive account of the problems with non-pro rata government programs, see Richard A. Epstein, *Takings: Private Property Under the Power of Eminent Domain* (Cambridge: Harvard University Press, 1985), esp. chaps. 14–18. See also idem, "Taxation, Regulation, and Confiscation," *Osgoode Hall Law Journal* 20 (1982): 433.

19. For an elaboration, see Richard A. Epstein, "Possession as the Root of Title," *Georgia Law Review* 13 (1979): 1221.

20. See John Finnis, *Natural Law and Natural Rights* (New York: Oxford University Press, 1980), 187 (emphasis in original).

21. See John Rawls, *A Theory of Justice* (Cambridge: Harvard University Press, 1971), in which the constant theme is that natural differences in talent are morally arbitrary. Thus Rawls notes: "Intuitively, the most obvious injustice of the system of natural liberty is that it permits distributive shares to be improperly influenced; by these factors so arbitrary from a moral point of view." Ibid., 72. The arbitrary factors include both natural and social contingencies, and "the cumulative effect of prior distributions of natural assets— that is, natural talents and abilities." Even if this system of natural liberties is enhanced by a system of equal access to opportunity, Rawls still believes it is imperfect, for "even if it works to perfection in eliminating the influence of social contingencies, it still permits the distribution of wealth and income to be determined by the natural distribution of abilities and talents." Ibid., 73–74. It is the effort to overcome the natural distribution that creates the common pool of human talents and its attendant political difficulties.

22. See, e.g., Clifford Holderness, "A Legal Foundation for Exchange," *Journal Legal Studies* 14 (1985): 321.

23. See Wellman, *Welfare Rights,* 111–12.

24. As an illustration see, e.g., Alvin E. Roth, "The Evolution of the Labor Market for Medical Interns and Residents: A Case Study in Game Theory," *Journal of Politics and Economics* 92 (1984): 991.

25. I develop this theme at great length in connection with the eminent domain clause in *Takings;* see also idem, "Toward a Revitalization of the Contract Clause," *University of Chicago Law Review* 51 (1984): 703.

26. For a review of Pareto superiority and Kaldor-Hicks (hypothetical compensation) tests, see Jules Coleman, "Economics and the Law: A Critical Review of the Foundations of the Economic Approach to Law," *Ethics* 94 (1984): 649.

27. See Wellman, *Welfare Rights,* 65.

28. Ibid., 65–66.

29. See generally, James M. Buchanan, Robert D. Tollison, and Gordon Tullock, eds., *Toward a Theory of the Rent-Seeking Society* (College Station: Texas A & M University, 1980). I have explored the process in constitutional discourse in "Toward a Revitalization of the Contract Clause."

30. Richard G. Lipsey and Peter O. Steiner, *Economics,* 6th ed. (New York: Harper & Row, 1981), 346.

31. See Wellman, *Welfare Rights,* 33–34.

32. Here the rent-seeking literature is of great importance. See generally, Buchanan, Tollison, and Tullock, *Toward a Theory of the Rent-Seeking Society*.

33. One piece of evidence on this point notes that with the increase in welfare programs today, the number of persons whose earnings are enough to keep themselves above the poverty line has declined with the increase in levels of welfare expenditures. The poverty totals have continued downward, but only at about the same rate of decline as before the massive increases in expenditures beginning in the Johnson years. For a discussion of this "latent" poverty, see Murray, *Losing Ground,* 64–65.

34. See generally Epstein, *Takings,* chap. 19, for a discussion of the problem, and the way in which voluntary charity is better able to cope with the incessant pressure to increase the size and scope of welfare programs.

35. The relation between utility and wealth may be stated as follows. Suppose each of ten persons filled his own basket with twenty dollars' worth of goods at the market. The total wealth would equal two hundred dollars. Yet, if someone took the baskets and assigned them to different persons, wealth would remain constant but utility would be diminished as much of the consumer surplus would be removed. In principle, if transaction costs were zero the baskets could all be reassigned to their original owners. But once transaction costs are positive, the levels of utility are reduced by the level of these costs, and could easily drop below two hundred dollars, as when all persons value what they now have less than the twenty dollars they paid to get it.

36. See John Rawls, *Theory of Justice,* 153, where Rawls offers his justification for the maximum solution: choose that set of possible outcomes with the highest minimum value, without regard to the probability of its occurrence or the gains foregone from other choices. At root only risk aversion (and a very strong form of risk aversion at that) can justify this choice.

37. The expression "veil of ignorance" is, of course, from Rawls, *Theory of Justice,* 136–42. The theory is that persons stripped of special knowledge will only be able to advance their personal welfare by advancing the general welfare. On Rawls, see generally Norman Daniels, ed., *Reading Rawls: Critical Studies on Rawls' A Theory of Justice* (New York: Basic Books, 1975).

The essay by Frank Michelman, "Constitutional Welfare Rights and *A Theory of Justice,*" in *Reading Rawls,* 319, and his earlier article upon which it was based, "In Pursuit of Constitutional Welfare Rights: One View of Rawls' Theory of Justice," *University of Pennsylvania Law Review* 121 (1973): 962, attempt to erect an argument that the Constitution, and in particular the due process and equal protection clauses of the Fourteenth Amendment create welfare rights. But the text of the Fourteenth Amendment itself seems far more congenial to the protection of rights against interference at common law. Historically, there is little reason to think that an amendment passed at the height of the laissez-faire era should be read as a mandate for extensive government welfare programs.

38. See, e.g. Murray, *Losing Ground,* and Gwartney and McCaleb, "Have Antipoverty Programs Increased Poverty?" which gather much of the data in an easily understood form.

39. Russell D. Roberts, "A Positive Model of Private Charity and Public Transfers," *Journal of Political Economy* 92 (Feb. 1984): 136.

40. See, e. g., Keeble v. Hickeringill, 11 East 574, 103 Eng. Rep. 1127, 1128 (K.B. 1809), and its discussion of a hypothetical case of a schoolmaster who loses his pupils when a rival blocks the way to his school with guns. See also Tarlton v. M'Gawley, 1 Peake 270, 170 Eng. Rep. 153 (K.B. 1793). For a collection of materials, see Richard A. Epstein, Charles O. Gregory, and Harry Kalven, Jr., *Cases and Materials on Torts,* 4th ed. (Boston: Little, Brown & Co., 1984), 1344–54.

III

THE "NEW" SCIENCE OF POLITICS AND CONSTITUTIONAL GOVERNMENT

★

Walter Berns

T he ninth *Federalist* does not merit the careful study political scientists have customarily devoted to the famous tenth; in truth, there is in it very little to study. Unlike the tenth, it consists not in profound political analysis but, rather, in a remarkable assertion, an assertion that, if given the attention it deserves, prepares the reader for the analysis that follows.

Hamilton begins by acknowledging that history seems to support the arguments advanced by "the advocates of despotism" to the effect that free republican government is an impossibility. There had been republics in the past, specifically the "petty republics of Greece and Italy"; and there had also been free governments—some of them "stupendous fabrics reared on the basis of liberty, which have flourished for ages." But the republics were

Walter Berns is John M. Olin University Professor at Georgetown University and an adjunct scholar at the American Enterprise Institute.

unstable, wracked by "tempestuous waves of sedition and party rage" which caused them to fluctuate "between the extremes of tyranny and anarchy"; and the free governments, while stable and sometimes even "glorious," were not republican in form (9:71–72). Nothing in this history gives comfort to the friends of republican government, and were it not for an unprecedented event in the world of science, they would be obliged to concede that the advocates of despotism were right.

> The science of politics, however, like most other sciences, has received great improvement [lately]. The efficacy of various principles is now well understood, which were either not known at all, or imperfectly known to the ancients. (72)

By adopting these principles in its Constitution, America could succeed where all other nations had failed: it could combine liberty and order under a republican form. That, I would submit, is a remarkable assertion.

No less remarkable, perhaps, is the character of these newly discovered principles. They are decidedly not educational principles. Aristotle, the founder of the old political science, could assert confidently that the education of the young requires the special attention of the lawgiver, and that this education had to be adapted to the particular form of constitution, by which he meant that the democratic constitution, for example, required a democratic education for its young.[1] But there is no reference in *Federalist* No. 9 to the education of republican citizens or anything having to do with civic virtue and how it might be promoted or fostered. These were the concerns of the old political science. The new political science is concerned not with the political material but with the structure of government; it had devised a model of "a more perfect structure," and had done so on the basis of principles "not known at all, or imperfectly known to the ancients" (72).

The elements of this structure are familiar to all students of American government: "The regular distribution of power into distinct departments; the introduction of legislative balances and checks; the institution of courts composed of judges holding their offices during good behavior; the representation of the people in the legislature by deputies of their own election," and last but not least, "the ENLARGEMENT of the ORBIT within which such systems are to revolve." These organizational principles are said to be the means "by which the excellencies of republican government may be retained and its imperfections lessened or avoided" (72–73). As I said, a remarkable assertion or claim, at the time perhaps even extravagant, but not so when viewed from the perspective supplied by almost two hundred years of unparalleled political prosperity. What the Framers of the U.S. Constitution came to understand through study and reflection we can confirm through experience: the new science of politics succeeded where the old had failed.

It may also be true, however, that it failed where the old had succeeded. Macaulay, the greatest of the Victorians, had something like this in mind when he contrasted the work of Plato and Francis Bacon, taking the former as the exemplar of the old philosophy and Bacon of the new.

> The aim of the Platonic philosophy was to raise us far above
> vulgar wants. The aim of the Baconian philosophy was to supply
> our vulgar wants. The former aim was noble; but the latter was
> attainable.[2]

Stated in political terms, the old philosophy described the path leading to the good and noble, which it defined; the new philosophy devised institutions facilitating the pursuit of happiness, which it allowed everyone to define for himself. Or, to put this in terms familiar to us all, we modern men want liberty, and mean by it the right to be left alone; and it is by no means obvious that the ancients wanted liberty, not in that sense. Therefore, the essential difference between the old and new political sciences is not in their respective institutions, although these are significant, but in their purpose. It is of some interest to note that this difference is reflected in our familiar political speech.

We speak of the Reagan (Carter, Roosevelt, Lincoln, Washington) administration and eschew the use of the term government, as in Thatcher (Churchill, Baldwin, Gladstone, Pitt) government, and only somewhat hidden in that usage is the idea that we, unlike the subjects of governments founded originally on older principles, are not governed. We govern ourselves, and our public officials administer. "Government," as Professor Storing put it in his last published work, is "no longer seen as directing and shaping human existence, but as having the much narrower (though indispensable) function of facilitating the peaceful enjoyment of the private life. In this view, government and the whole public sphere are decisively instrumental; government is reduced to administration."[3] Hence, as I say, we speak of the Reagan and Washington administrations.

By not being governed, I mean we are not ruled, and it is a fact that we eschew the use of the term ruler as well. We sometimes speak of leaders, as in political leaders, but leaders are part of us; we appoint or choose them to lead us where *we* want to go. Our curricula sometimes list courses in political leadership, and political scientists write books under that title; but there are no courses or new books on ruling. So pervasive has been the influence of this modern and, in essence, democratic usage, that even tyrants are referred to as leaders (*Führer, Duce*).

But the old political science spoke of ruling. It did so because the various elements constituting the political community—the people (or the poor), the aristocracy (or the rich), the legitimate, the holy, or whatever—each claimed a right to rule, and to do so on the basis of its characteristic principle. "Ruling," as Professors Kurland and Lerner have put it, "rests on a claim by a part of the body politic to govern the whole according to that part's distinctive opinion of what is just."[4] These claims—the people (or the free) should rule, the rich should rule, the virtuous should rule— are mutually exclusive, if not incompatible with each other; each rests on a different opinion of justice; each implies an understanding of what is good for the particular society and, as well, an understanding of what is the good society simply. According to Aristotle (the founder of the old political science), every society, or regime, derives its distinctive character from the opinion of justice held by its ruling part. A society ruled by the rich, or the holy, or by a hereditary monarch, would differ distinctively from one ruled by the people.

It was understood to be the task of political science to weigh or evaluate these various and clashing opinions of what constitutes the good regime, and this evaluation culminated in a description of the best regime. Which is to say, it culminated in a definition of the good life and the political arrangements appropriate to it.

As Macaulay said of the Platonic philosophy, its aim "was to raise us far above vulgar wants."

There was no expectation that the best regime might be realized in practice, or, for that matter, closely approximated; at most, it was hoped that it might serve as a model. Aristotle's most practicable regime, which he refers to simply as "polity," and which in our texts is given the name "mixed" or balanced government, amounts to rule by the middle class. It is a blend—achieved, for example, by a modest property qualification—of democracy and oligarchy, or of the claims of the poor and those of the rich, and undertaken with a view to moderating these claims in practice. Not only is the middle class that rules more moderate than the partisan elements of which it is composed—it is not inclined to deprive the people of their liberty or the rich of their property—but its very moderation might dispose it in favor of virtue. And insofar as the old political science focused our attention on virtue, it can be said to have succeeded precisely where the new has failed. It is worth noting that the old political science led to the building of universities devoted to humane studies, and the new political science led to the building of business schools. Unfortunately, as Kurland and Lerner say, "in practice, the properly mixed or balanced rule of partisans has seldom if ever appeared outside the pages of Aristotle," a fact duly noted in *Federalist* No. 9. The "history of the petty republics of Greece and Italy," we are told, reveals occasional moments of "calm" and even of "felicity," but these are soon "overwhelmed by the tempestuous waves of sedition and party rage" (71–72). By party rage, Hamilton, the author of *Federalist* No. 9, meant the rage of partisans who claimed the right to rule the whole. The new political science hoped to rid the "city," or the country, of this sort of partisan, or of partisanship in this sense, or of what Tocqueville was later to call "great parties."[5] It hoped to do this by abolishing ruling in favor of representation.

The new political science can be said to have originated in the seventeenth century, a time of intense partisanship in Britain, so intense that Thomas Hobbes was led to conclude that the natural condition of men resembled a state of war wherein life was solitary, poor, nasty, brutish, and short. The most radical party was the king's, for the king claimed to rule by divine grace: *dei gratia, rex*. When this claim was supported by political science, in the person of Sir Robert Filmer, who traced the king's title to God's donation to Adam, John Locke responded with his *Two Treatises of Government*. The first of these is devoted to refuting Filmer, while the second is an account of the true "rise of government [or] original of political power,"[6] and, so far as the United States is concerned, the first statement of the new political science.

In it we learn that by nature *no* one is entitled to rule, that by nature all men are perfectly free and equal, that, viewed in the light of nature, all claims to rule are arbitrary and unfounded, which means there can be no political science respecting them, or no scientific evaluation of them. Government is necessary but arises only out of the contract entered into by these free and equal individuals; by this contract they consent to government. "The only way whereby any one divests himself of his natural liberty and puts on the bonds of civil society," Locke writes, "is by agreeing with other men to join and unite into a community for their comfortable, safe, and peaceable living one amongst another, in a secure enjoyment of their properties and a greater security against any that are not of it."[7] The true, or only just "rise of government" is consent.

But why should men surrender their natural right to govern themselves or divest themselves of their natural liberty "to order their actions and dispose of their possessions and persons as they see fit . . . without asking leave or depending upon the will of any other man"? The answer is, out of fear, out of a desire for security; for, while they possess certain rights by nature, these rights are insecure in nature. "[T]o avoid this state of war," as Locke (like Hobbes) puts it, "is one great reason of men's putting themselves into society and quitting the state of nature."[8] Or, in the words of our Declaration of Independence, "To secure these rights, Governments are instituted among men, deriving their just powers from the consent of the governed."

Still, the question recurs: Why should men give up their desire to rule or enslave others, to pursue glory by enlisting the aid of others, to build a society of saints or public temples dedicated to virtue? The new political science had somehow to persuade men to forgo these dreams or subordinate these conflicting desires; it had to persuade them that what they have in common is more important than what divides them; that they share a common vulnerability and a common desire and need for peace or, as the Constitution's preamble puts it, for domestic tranquility. By aiming too high, or asking too much, they divide themselves into warring factions, either because they cannot agree on the objects of such desires (not everyone agrees with Bach that "Jesu [is the proper] Joy of Man's Desiring") or because the satisfying of one desire is incompatible with the satisfying of another. They have to come to agree with Macaulay that "an acre in Middlesex is better than a principality in Utopia,"[9] or with Locke that the "great and chief end . . . of men's uniting into commonwealths and putting themselves under government is the preservation of their property," by which he meant "their lives, liberties, and estates."[10]

Modern government is limited government, limited most of all in its purposes. Representative government is limited government because it does not represent the claims of "great parties," parties led by a Charles I, a Cromwell, a Napoleon, a Guelph or Ghibelline or nobleman, or a Lenin or Hitler; it represents what can safely be represented, and what can be safely represented are particular versions of concerns held in common. Who is to be represented? Or as Madison puts it in *Federalist* No. 57, "Who are to be the electors of federal representatives?"

> Not the rich, more than the poor; not the learned, more than
> the ignorant; not the haughty heirs of distinguished names,
> more than the humble sons of obscure and unpropitious fortune.
> The electors are to be the great body of the people of the United
> States. (351)

And what do the people of the United States have in common? The desire to secure their rights, their *equal* rights. And what is it that divides them? Not, as in the past, their conflicting views of justice, not a disagreement as to who should rule, not their differing visions of the good life; such visions have been made politically irrelevant, taken out of politics, so to speak, removed from the public sphere to the private. As I said earlier with reference to the Declaration of Independence, men are endowed by nature's God with the right to pursue happiness as they individually define it. What is it, then, that divides them? Merely their interests, and, so far as politics is concerned, primarily their economic interests. As Madison says in *Federalist* No. 10, "the regulation of these various and interfering interests forms the principal task of modern legislation" (79). It was thought that regulating economic interests would be a much less formidable task than adjusting claims to rule.

In this context it should be noted that the task of regulating these interests is to be performed by the representatives of the interests themselves. Representatives do not come to the seat of government bearing petitions from their constituents to be laid at the feet of some ruler. On the contrary, they, themselves, in Congress assembled, make the decisions.

To summarize: "the representation of the people in the legisla-ture by deputies of their own election" (72) was said in *Federalist* No. 9 to be one of the wholly new discoveries made by the new political science, and I have tried to explain what is new about it. In a word, representation, whose foundations were laid by Locke and whose principles were adopted by the Founders of the United States, "was developed in response to the ancient notion of rule."[11] Representation is a substitute for ruling in the sense that, according to this new dispensation, men do not claim a right to rule but only to be represented.

As Madison argues in *Federalist* Nos. 10 and 63, representation is also a substitute for pure democracy, a system in which the people "assemble and administer the government in person" (10:81). By refining and enlarging "the public views by passing them through the medium of a chosen body of citizens," it might, and under certain conditions it will, promote the public good better than if "the people themselves, convened for the purpose." It would, however, be of no avail in a small republic. There, within the limited confines of a small territory and small population, candidates might become popular by practicing the "vicious arts by which elections are too often carried," and then use that popularity to betray the interests of the people. In saying this, Madison has in mind bribery and demagoguery. Or, on the other hand, they might simply serve as tools of local factions and prejudices. Representation will work well only in a large repub-lic, or within the enlarged orbit, another of the discoveries of the new science of politics. The large republic will permit larger districts, thus making available a larger number of fit candidates and making it more difficult for "unworthy candidates to practice with success [those] vicious arts" (82); and, secondly, the larger the district, the greater the variety of interests, thus reducing the representative's dependence on any particular one. And, of course, the larger the country, the greater the variety of interests, thus making "it less probable that a majority of the whole will have a common motive to invade the rights of other citizens" (83). Districting is the key to proper representation. Districting makes possible the representation of the variety of local interests and prevents representation *"of the people in their collective capacity"* (63:387). The alternative to electing representatives by districts is electing them at large, and thereby representing them in their collective capacity. At-large elections would, in their consequences, resemble a pure democracy: they would facilitate the building of a majority faction and thereby place the rights of the minority in jeopardy.

In making this argument for an enlarged orbit, the Federalists were opposing one of the venerable principles of the old political science, namely, that republican government was possible only within a "contracted territory" composed of a small population. This argument was made repeatedly by the Antifederalists during the ratification debates. The Federalists opposed it because, among other reasons, they did not subscribe to the principle, shortly to be made popular by Jeremy Bentham, of the greatest good of the greatest number. They suspected that the rights of all could not be secured in a system allowing the greatest number— or a simple majority of the people—to have their way. That, more or less, was the system prevailing in the various states from which, Madison says in *Federalist* No. 10, "complaints are everywhere heard from our most considerate and virtuous citizens . . . that measures are too often decided, not according to the rules of justice and the rights of the minor party, but by the superior force of an interested and overbearing majority" (77).

Most to be feared was a majority hostile to the rights of property; such a majority, resentful of the wealth enjoyed by the few, had somehow to be prevented from ruling, and, if allowed to gain control of the government, *rule* it most surely would. Thus, the Constitutional Convention discussed the propriety and possibility of meeting the challenge by imposing a property qualification on voting or somehow representing property as well as numbers of people.[12] In the end, however, the Convention simply adopted the least restrictive of the voter qualifications in force in the states, which meant that the challenge posed by a resentful majority—or faction, to adopt Madison's term—had to be met in some other way. The system of representation was only a partial answer. Of what use would it be if in this large republic there were to be not a great variety of interests but, for example, a united working class, a proletariat, with one interest, the "forcible overthrow of all existing social conditions?"[13] What assurance did the Founders have that Americans would not be divided into two great parties, one of the rich and one of the poor, rather than into a multiplicity of interests?

Here again they relied on the new political science developed by John Locke, that and the fact that at the time most Americans were not hostile to the idea of private property and the right to acquire it. Madison was apparently so confident of this that he could write—and in a very public place, a newspaper—that the first object of government is "the protection of different and unequal faculties of acquiring property" (10:78). From the protection of these unequal faculties would come (and, as we know, did come) not only different "kinds" of property, but "different degrees" of property. It is almost as if Madison were arguing that the first object of government is to promote an unequal distribution of wealth.

Yet, his statement is wholly in accord with the principle, stated in the Declaration of Independence, that the purpose of government is to secure the rights of all. Madison is acknowledging the fact that the only respect in which men are equal is in their possession of rights; they are not equally endowed with intelligence, energy, diligence, pertinacity, or any of the other faculties from which, as he says, "the [civil] rights of property originate" (78). To secure everyone's natural right to acquire property is to secure the rights of otherwise unequally endowed men, and thereby ensure that some become rich and that others remain poor, or relatively poor. But it also promotes economic development, and this was Madison's point. By assuring the "industrious and rational" (Locke's term)[14] that they may earn all they can and keep much of what they rightfully earn, the country inspires enterprise and stands to profit from it. In fact, it inspires almost everybody to be enterprising,[15] causing a growth in the common wealth. If Locke was right, and subsequent experience proves that he was, wealth would increase by a factor of a thousand and more.[16] This would have salutary political consequences. As is always and everywhere the case, the wealth would be unevenly distributed, but our rich (unlike the rich of the past) would have no interest in keeping the poor down, and our poor (unlike the poor of the past) would have no interest in bringing the rich down. The exception to this, and it serves to prove the rule, would be in the feudal South where the life of the whites depended on their being able to keep the blacks down and whose destiny was to be brought down by the blacks.[17]

To summarize: in addition to making it possible to realize the benefits of representation, the enlarged orbit would promote economic prosperity; it would do for the United States from the beginning what western Europe with its common market has been trying to do for the last quarter century. It would enlarge the opportunities for the "industrious and rational" and might even cause "the quarrelsome and contentious" (again, Locke's term) to realize that they would be better off by going to work. Hamilton states this well in *Federalist* No. 12:

> By multiplying the means of gratification, by promoting the introduction and circulation of the precious metals, those darling objects of human avarice and enterprise, [the prosperity of commerce] serves to vivify and invigorate all the channels of industry and to make them flow with greater activity and copiousness. The assiduous merchant, the laborious husbandman, the active mechanic, and the industrious manufacturer—all orders of men look forward with eager expectation and growing alacrity to this pleasing reward of their toils. (91)

"The prosperity of commerce," as Hamilton says in the same paragraph, "is now perceived and acknowledged by all enlightened statesmen to be the most useful as well as the most productive source of national wealth, and has accordingly become a primary object of their political cares." A few years before this was written Rousseau had deplored the fact that while "the ancient political thinkers talked incessantly about morals and virtue, those of our time talk only of commerce and money."[18]

Their reason for doing so was not, ultimately, to promote the material wealth of nations; their object, and the American Founders' object, was constitutional or limited government. By taking government out of the business of promoting morals and virtue, to use Rousseau's terms, they expected material gratification, or comfortable preservation, to emerge as the primary object of men's passions. In the past, governments had in one way or another attempted to suppress these passions, but the commercial republic would be built on them. The authors of the *Federalist* had learned from Montesquieu (whom they repeatedly referred to as "the celebrated Montesquieu") that commerce cures destructive prejudices, that it "softens barbaric morals," that it causes men to lose their taste for personal glory or conquest or desire for salvation, or any of the other things giving rise to disruptive factions.[19] It makes men "soft," but it makes constitutional government possible. The pursuit of wealth can, of course, divide a society between the rich and the poor, but when, thanks to the new political economy, every man has a reasonable expectation of achieving some measure of wealth and comfort, and the safety they bring, this traditional hostility will be muted. Men will be characterized by their interests, and these interests are not mutually incompatible. To state this in the language of *Federalist* No. 10, in the large commercial republic, the animosity of factions will become the competition of interests, and this competition will be peaceful.

With the principles discovered or perfected by the new science of politics—separation of powers, checks and balances, an independent judiciary, as well as those treated in this essay—the Founders hoped to lay the foundation for a strong and stable government under which men are free to pursue their own view of happiness, without fear of their neighbors or foreign enemies. Washington gave eloquent voice to this hope in 1790 in his answer to an "Address" from the Hebrew Congregation of Newport, Rhode Island:

> It is now no more that tolerance is spoken of, as if it was by the indulgence of one class of people, that another enjoyed the exercise of their inherent natural rights. For happily the government of the United States, which gives to bigotry no sanction, to persecution no assistance, requires only that they who live under its protection should demean themselves as good citizens, in giv-

ing it on all occasions their effectual support. . . . May the children of the Stock of Abraham, who dwell in this land, continue to merit and enjoy the good will of the other inhabitants, while everyone shall sit in safety under his own vine and fig-tree, and there shall be none to make him afraid.[20]

Notes

1. Aristotle *Politics* 8.1337a10–19.

2. Thomas B. Macaulay, "Francis Bacon," in *Critical and Historical Essays* vol. 2 (London: J. M. Dent & Sons, Everyman's Library, 1951), 373.

3. Herbert J. Storing, "American Statesmanship: Old and New," in *Bureaucrats, Policy Analysts, Statesmen: Who Leads?* (Washington, D.C.: American Enterprise Institute, 1980), 97.

4. Philip B. Kurland and Ralph Lerner, "Representation," in *The Founder's Constitution,* vol. 1, (Chicago: University of Chicago Press, 1987), chap. 13.

5. Alexis de Tocqueville, *Democracy in America,* vol. 1, ed. Phillips Bradley (New York: Alfred A. Knopf, 1972), pt. 2, chap. 2.

6. John Locke, *Two Treatises of Government,* sec. 1.

7. Ibid., sec. 95.

8. Ibid., sec. 21.

9. Macaulay, "Francis Bacon."

10. Locke, *Treatises,* secs. 123, 124.

11. Kurland and Lerner, *The Founder's Constitution.*

12. Jefferson seems to have thought this appropriate. See *Notes on the State of Virginia,* Query 13.

13. Karl Marx, *Manifesto of the Communist Party.*

14. Locke, *Treatises,* sec. 34.

15. As Tocqueville wrote his father on first landing in America, "Everybody works, and the mine is so rich that all those who work rapidly succeed in acquiring that which renders existence happy." George W. Pierson, *Tocqueville and Beaumont in America* (New York: Oxford University Press, 1938), 115.

16. In the chapter on property, Locke begins by suggesting that God's providence is bountiful, and in support of this quotes 1 Timothy 6:17: "God has given us all things richly." He then, very subtly, suggests that by adopting his principles of political economy this original "bounty" can be increased tenfold, a hundredfold, a thousandfold, and ends up by saying the original gift was "almost worthless." See Locke, *Treatises,* secs. 26, 31, 34, 37, 41, 42.

17. Tocqueville, upon crossing the river from Ohio to Kentucky, commented on the difference between the two economies in a letter to his father:

> For the first time we have had a chance to examine there the effect that slavery produces on society. On the right bank of the Ohio everything is activity, indus-

try; labour is honored; there are no slaves. Pass to the left bank and the scene changes so suddenly that you think yourself on the other side of the world; the enterprising spirit is gone. There, work is not only painful; it's shameful, and you degrade yourself in submitting yourself to it. To ride, to hunt, to smoke like a Turk in the sunshine: there is the destiny of the White. (Pierson, *Tocqueville*, 582.)

18. Jean-Jacques Rousseau, "Discours sur les Sciences et les Arts," in *Oeuvres Complètes*, vol. 3 (Paris: Pléiades, 1964), 19.

19. Montesquieu, *Esprit des Lois* 1.10.1. See Thomas L. Pangle, *Montesquieu's Philosophy of Liberalism: A Commentary on "The Spirit of the Laws"* (Chicago: University of Chicago Press, 1973), 203–9.

20. Address by George Washington to the Hebrew Congregation of Newport, August 1790, in *Writings*, vol. 31, ed. John C. Fitzpatrick (Washington, D.C.: Government Printing Office, 1931–44), 93n.

IV

CONSTITUTIONALISM AND THE RULE OF LAW

★

Noel B. Reynolds

The bicentennial of the Constitution of the United States of America invites our reflection on the extraordinary historical success of this document and its attendant institutions. In the history of mankind, it stands alone as the most successful of the sustained experiments in human freedom and self-government.

Such reflections may take on some urgency when we note the reduced level of basic constitutional wisdom which prevails among both the politicians, who are most directly responsible for maintaining the Constitution, and the political theorists, who provide our political culture with its self-understanding. It seems that the eighteenth century may have seen the high tide of such understanding in the western world. And the American Founders were without peer in their own day.

In this essay I attempt to articulate the underlying principles which account for the success of the American constitutional experiment and indeed for similar freedoms that have been achieved in different degrees and for varying lengths of time in human polities throughout the world. The same analysis, by

Noel Reynolds is a Professor of Political Science at Brigham Young University.

contrast, will serve to illuminate failures to achieve freedom elsewhere.

One indication of the decline in understanding of these matters over the last century occurs in the current edition of an authoritative reference work. The author announces somewhat disdainfully that "constitutionalism is the name given to the trust which men repose in the power of words engrossed on parchment to keep a government in order."[1] Armed with such a narrow definition, it is no wonder that the author is able to insist that "the rise of constitutionalism may be dated from 1776."[2] From this most unpromising beginning the author goes on to develop a cynical account of the means by which clever lawyers and judges transform the doctrines of the Constitution over time to make of the document a useful instrument of social control. As if the Constitution had been intended as a repository or oracle for doctrines to settle all future questions of fundamental law! The appalling ignorance reflected in this authoritative source is only one indication of the widespread dearth of constitutionalist wisdom.

As difficult as some of our contemporaries seem to make the understanding of human freedom, we can find numerous historical examples of its achievement within the framework of rule of law and constitutional devices. This is important because it emphasizes the universality of the solutions which were perfected by the American Founders.

PRIMITIVE SOCIETIES

Rule of law through constitutional government is a recurring solution to an ageless problem in human societies, the problem of controlling the rulers. That there should be no rulers or government is a thought comprehensible only to a few theorists locked away in their ivory towers. That rulers need to be restrained has been the eventual discovery of every society. Constitutionalism is the science of such restraints.

Because of their distance from modern society, primitive cultures are often used to identify the universal elements of human societies. Studies of primitive political systems reveal constitutional arrangements which are designed to prevent the emergence of any single individual or group as a tyrant, while simultaneously providing for the necessary government to make orderly and beneficial decisions for communal action.

Our primitive brothers have access to one important control on their authorities that we have lost in modern secularized society— the requirement that they maintain the approval of the gods. The disapproval of the gods can be discovered by councils of priests consulting oracles or interpreting natural or social events. As one might expect, there are always very practical sanctions available to supplement the theological sanction of divine disapproval.

In most primitive societies, political power is balanced and authority is distributed for the various kinds of community decisions which must be made. Councils are used in most cases to provide representative decisions. Elaborate rituals of rebellion are enacted annually in some monarchical societies to remind the king of his dependence on the support of the people. And without exception, kings, chiefs, and councils are not authorized to change the laws and customs of the people. Furthermore, they are required to enforce those laws and customs and to obey them in the conduct of their own affairs. The common wisdom of primitive man seems to be that law or rules must also govern the rulers.

It might be thought that these primitive constitutional arrangements are ageless as they occur in different societies. This common western belief proves to be a myth as observers note the ongoing shifting of such arrangements in almost all such societies. Primitive peoples have never been immune to the dynamic forces of nature and society that impose continual change on their conditions of life. Wars, plagues, famines, and migrations disturb the important power balances that have been developed, requiring that new arrangements emerge.

Lucy Mair's studies of this process of change would support the conclusion that in times of constitutional failure, primitive peoples naturally adapt previously nonpolitical organizational elements of their societies to restructure their political system and regain constitutional balance.[3] This is not to assert that such experimentation never misfires. But the politicization of social clubs or councils and the transformation of functions of existing political institutions goes on endlessly in the quest to balance power and authority within a continually changing society. The suggestion for us is that the constitutional problem is an endless one never to be resolved once and for all.

For example, the Iroquois suffered a major historical crisis when their ill-fated alliance with the English in the Revolutionary War forced them to leave the United States. Originally the Iroquois had no central government but only a ceremonial council of fifty chiefs. Because the English would only deal with the Iroquois through a single authoritative leader in the making of treaties, the Iroquois responded by conferring upon the council more and more specialized political functions and claiming for that council a monopoly of the representative right in dealings with the British. As time went on other problems emerged. The fur supply declined and the Iroquois resorted to war with distant Indian tribes to protect their control of the fur trade. To maintain these wars, standing war chiefs were established. The British government first gave the Iroquois a Canadian endowment which embraced twelve thousand square miles, but they were later forced onto a vastly smaller seventy-square-mile reservation. Again the council responded with the development of specialized offices. A welfare chief was appointed, then a forest warden, and so forth.[4]

Succession is a central constitutional problem, especially in the well-defined kingship systems of many African tribes. Hilda Kuper found the constitutional arrangements of the Swazi of South Africa focused on a form of dual monarchy in which the king, or Great Lion, shared every prerogative with his mother.[5] The queen mother, or Lady Elephant, had her own courts, counselors, and troops, as well as some authority over the king. The queen mother actually functioned as a court of appeal and would be replaced by her own sister or daughter should she die. In addition to the balance of the dual monarchy, there were permanent councils composed of the heads of the various lineages that were also involved in decision making with the king.

Rituals of rebellion have been observed among certain African tribes and the Natchez Indians of Louisiana. Max Gluckman reports that the king of the Zulu was required to make an annual wandering through the villages of his kingdom naked and without arms or supplies.[6] As he appeared in each village he would be persecuted and even threatened with spears and abused with language ordinarily reserved for the most vile members of this society. This ritual reminds a king of the precariousness of his position and that a real rebellion may lead both to his death and his replacement. If in fact he returns safely from the tour, he resumes his kingly regalia, receives the praise of his people, and is reinstated in his position. But he has been sharply warned that he must always remember to seek the welfare of his people.

CLASSICAL CONSTITUTIONALISM

The failure to see the antiquity of constitutionalism is directly related to the failure to see this institutional balancing of the social decision-making process as its essence. Constitutional thought, in this sense, was explicitly developed among the ancient Greeks and Romans, as evidenced not only in the writings of Plato, Aristotle, Polybius, and others, but also in political institutions over a period of many centuries. It seems clear that Plato saw that a primary function of government was to protect and maintain the law of the people.[7] He furthermore explicitly discussed the various institutional designs that might be used to achieve this, namely monarchy, aristocracy, and democracy. His almost casual, yet sophisticated, treatment of these concepts betrays his assumption that his contemporary audience understood these matters completely and that little detailed explanation was necessary. As Plato went on to name the corrupted forms of his three constitutional regimes, he clearly saw the source of corruption in their failure to maintain the rule of law as they fell into tyrannical practices. Plato was not an optimist; he seemed to believe that each of the good regimes bore within itself the seeds of its own destruction—a view of all worldly constitutions which Bentham echoed in the nineteenth century, asserting that only the Constitution of the Anglo-American United States "affords a reasonable promise of everlasting endurance."[8]

Because Plato wrote in dialogue form, his views in these matters are not as apparent as those of his student, Aristotle, who used the philosophical treatise. To Plato's notion of a general cycling through the different regimes and their corruptions, Aristotle added the idea of mixed government wherein the democratic, aristocratic, and monarchical elements of the state could be mixed into one regime which could have the potential for sustained balance of constitutional power. The Aristotelian idea of mixed government formed the basis for classical constitutional theory in conjunction with the commitment to the principle of rule of law.[9] The idea was revived and revitalized in modern Europe, particularly England, and even served as a guiding ideal to the American Founding Fathers, who struggled with the problem of institutional balancing in a society which did not have an aristocracy or a monarch.

Plato and Aristotle were writing within a tradition that had long treasured law and the principle of rule of law. The early Greeks credited their laws to their divine ancestors and therefore gave no earthly mortal a right to change those laws. The ancient poet, Pindar, expressed that Greek view: "The law is king of all."[10] In the early history of the Athenian constitution the commitment to law was a constant. Over time, a wide variety of political institutions emerged to secure and maintain that law, including monarchy, aristocracy, and democracy. Even though none of these had authority to change the ancient law it was under constant revision through one or another process of interpretation. But as late as the fifth century the Athenians maintained constitutional watch-dog bodies that could punish a magistrate for acting beyond his legal authority.

We know more about the law of ancient Rome, but find in it the same type of constitutional commitments used by the Greeks. Private law was the original source for all Roman law. The public law, as it developed, was conceived as a form of generalized private contract. Government structures were developed over time explicitly to maintain and enforce the law. This pattern is strikingly analogous to that of English common law centuries later. But as time went on and the Romans enjoyed international success, they had to adapt their law to imperial circumstances. They adopted new fictions which allowed the emperor to announce the will of the people, the recognized ultimate basis of all Roman law.

The later reputation of Roman absolutism unjustly descends from this Justinian formulation. But the true Roman doctrine, which was reasserted in the Middle Ages, was that the populace is the source of all law and that any public law, and especially any tax, must be based on consent. One of the great twentieth-century scholars of constitutionalism, Charles H. McIlwain, concluded that "whatever our modern laws may be, Rome is the source of our jurisprudence, and whatever our form of government, Greece has furnished us the main outlines of our political science."[11]

MEDIEVAL CONSTITUTIONALISM

The constitutional struggles of the Middle Ages were carried on at two different but interrelated levels. On the international level, the popes struggled with the emperors and the kings, while on the national level, kings struggled with their own people. The story is far too long and too complicated to be even summarized here beyond noting that, with respect to the papal struggles, the kings eventually won the right of approval for the appointment of bishops as well as the right to rule over the bishops within their territory.[12] Furthermore, as a concession to the secular authorities, the selection of popes was finally regularized by a rule requiring the agreement of two-thirds of all the cardinals. The papal argument that all legitimate political authority is derived from and subject to the pope, and the view that all material goods in the world are ultimately owned by the pope so that all earthly rulers are stewards to the pope—as advanced in its latest form in 1301 by Giles of Rome—were ultimately overthrown.

John of Paris produced the most important constitutional analysis of the age. He responded to this logical and perverse extreme, arguing that the pope is only a steward for the Christian community and its properties. Following Aquinas, he saw in civil government intrinsic dignity without any claim to ecclesiastical derivations, and concluded, therefore, in favor of a meaningful separation of church and state as a matter of constitutional arrangement. John justified popes in their spiritual censuring of kings and encouraged the deposition of wicked monarchs. But kings, he thought, could assist the cardinals in deposing an evil pope by force of arms! John was successful in bringing to the constitutional theory of the Middle Ages a view which was consonant with developments within the individual kingdoms. The best government in both church and state is representative and responsible to the people and protective of their laws.

The classic doctrine of a mixed state died out as a political institution during the Middle Ages except in the Italian republics. Yet, the idea was kept very much alive in literature as medieval writers tended to recall the successes of the Roman Republic. Aquinas argued that mixed government was the form of rule provided by God for the Israelites. John of Paris continued the defense of mixed government in his constitutional writings. The anti-papal writers in the Conciliar controversy even went so far as to argue that the church should develop a form of mixed government. And finally, the Renaissance writers such as Machiavelli and Erasmus succeeded in making the notion of a mixed state commonplace, even though the medieval pattern was kingship in almost every country.

The dualistic nature of medieval kingship probably resulted from the military organization of the Teutonic tribes in the early Middle Ages. The kings, as military leaders, held personal rule; and the business of government devolved upon the king as part of his household responsibilities. Every subject was personally tied to his king with a bond of allegiance.

As the story is very similar throughout Europe, the English experience can be representative. Before the advent of feudalism, vast areas of life in England were organized without any reference to the king. Land was owned outright by allodial tenure. The kings did not even enjoy the right of taxation until the tenth century. And folk courts carried the responsibility for law enforcement, serving almost like private arbitration boards or tribunals. Clearly, the political function of the king was extremely limited and the law of the people was the primary source of social control.

The early feudal kings attempted to redefine their political relationship to their subjects in terms of a divided land title and to convert kingship into a legal office. The late medieval struggles between the kings and the barons resulted in kings retaining position as personal rulers entitled to personal allegiance—but with limited power. Property retained its traditional autonomy so that taxation never became a royal right, but took the form of a voluntary grant given through parliament to the king. By virtue of his office, the king assumed responsibility for the administration of the law, but his judges could only enforce the existing rules and analogies of land law. They could not carry out new, conflicting, orders of the king.

Scholars have attempted a variety of analyses to explain this form of limited monarchy that occurred in these middle centuries. The English jurist, John Fortescue, saw this as a combination of "royal and constitutional rule," or, in other words, a monarchy in which the king ruled and made laws only with the assent of his subjects. Fortescue used this constitutional feature to distinguish between the royal rule of France and the limited monarchy of England.

One modern scholar of medieval political theory treats the same idea under the rubric of "double majesty."[13] Gierke believed the various theories of double majesty emerged as means of imposing limits on kings. But in the Middle Ages, two of these were most prominent—both deriving from Roman sources. It was characteristic of medieval writers to assert natural or universal law as a limitation on the prince. This ancient Stoic view had some influence, especially with philosophers at different times. But the more compelling legal view was the notion that law and the right to rule derive from the people in accordance with the ancient principles of Roman law.

McIlwain prefers to use Bracton's medieval distinction between *gubernaculum,* the king's unlimited sphere of action, and *jurisdictio,* that sphere within which the king is bound by law, whether it be natural law or custom.[14] The Achilles' heel of limited government in England was the absence of an institutional device that could restrain the king. What could the barons do when the king exceeded the understood limits? History shows that rebellion was their only real alternative. The confrontation of John at Runnymede—resulting in the Magna Charta—was only one of many such occasions in this general period.

McIlwain explains the breakdown of the medieval constitution as the outcome of a long struggle between monarchs and subjects to extend their respective spheres of government at the expense of the other. The tide of royal despotism crested in the sixteenth century with the royal promotion of doctrines of unlimited obedience to kings and of divine right of kings. This trend came to a head in the early seventeenth century with James I's assertion that the liberties of the people were not a matter of right, but of royal grant.

McIlwain does not believe that constitutional limitation could have survived had it not been for several unique characteristics of English political and legal life. The incredible toughness of English common law proved adequate to resist the royal attack. Determined English judges in the late sixteenth century refused to obey explicit orders from the monarch on the ground that they were of no force being "against the law of the land," and got away with it until the Stuarts gained control. The religious schisms of the times led dissenters, most notably Puritans, to revive old hostilities toward tyranny, bringing the defenders of law into an alliance with the schismatics against the expanding prerogative of the crown.

Although Parliament had not yet come into existence as an independent institution, defenders of law such as Coke and Wentworth asserted as early as 1621 that Parliament was the voice of the people—the essential premise of government on the Roman legal model. As the courts began to cave in to the Stuart monarchs, giving them discretion to make *gubernaculum* supreme over *jurisdictio,* double majesty was abandoned and revolution appeared to be the only course left open to the parliamentarians. How else could they deal with the star chamber denials of due process and the extraparliamentary tax assessments?

Modern Constitutionalism

Francis Wormuth has given us an outstanding analysis of the twenty years of constitutional speculation spawned by the English civil wars.[15] The Cromwellian years were characterized by experimentation and discussion of constitutionalist ideas including popular sovereignty, written constitutions, constitutional limitations, separation of powers, checks and balances, and bicameralism, among many other principles and institutional devices. Though written at this early date, James Harrington's *Oceana* served as a major inspiration for the American Founders, and notably John Adams. Many of the constitutional ideas which later came to fruition in the American experience first had a serious hearing in England at this time. But they were largely premature and unsuccessful in their own time.

With the demise of the Commonwealth in 1659, monarchy returned to England. Republican thinking was not eliminated, but was preserved more in the principles than in the institutions of politics. The Glorious Revolution formalized this arrangement in 1688, bringing to an end once and for all the claims of English monarchs to any absolute right of rule. Unfortunately, there was not sufficient foresight to provide against Parliament's filling the vacuum.

There is little doubt that eighteenth-century America was the setting for the historical high point of constitutionalism. Never before or probably since have such broad segments of a single population understood and valued the essential principles of the rule of law and the notion that the arrangement of political institutions can best serve as the fundamental device for protecting the law from tyrannical governors.

It is a commentary on our own times that we so frequently misrepresent the intellectual views of the men who produced the Constitution of 1787. A few years ago I had the opportunity of conversing at some length with a noted English historian and political theorist who made some comments on the American Revolution and Constitution. But his account sounded more like a description of the French experience after 1789. With some gentle probing I established to my dismay that my friend actually believed that the American Constitution features abstract announcements of natural law principles, and that the basic rationale used by the Americans for declaring their independence was an appeal to nature and political theory. He was astonished and even somewhat incredulous as I explained that at no point does the American Constitution advance any principle of natural law or political theory, that it only specifies the respective functions of and limitations on the various governmental agencies which it creates, and that the Revolution itself was quite deliberately justified in terms of the violation of the colonists' *legal* rights as Englishmen by the Crown in abuse of its lawful authority. The opening sentence of the Declaration announcing that all men are created equal cannot outweigh all the rest. It is certainly true that the American Founders did hold ideologies which included various principles of natural and divine law. But their constitutional documents do not mention these, and certainly do not rest on them directly as did the French parallels.

The debates over the American Constitution provide us with some of the best discussions of the basic rationale for constitutionalist theory, and James Madison provided the clearest and most widely used examples of that rationale.[16] Scholars are at least partially correct in tracing the intellectual inspiration of American political thinkers to such writers as Locke, Montesquieu, and the English radicals. But they are only now coming to realize the extent to which the Scottish philosophers, and particularly David Hume, produced the theoretical insights which guided the Founders. The Constitution is not a Lockean contract. Rather, it is an attempt, in the American context, to achieve the kind of institutional balancing and protection of law so esteemed by Hume in his *History of England* and *Political Essays*.[17] One author has found throughout Madison's and Hamilton's writings repeated references and borrowings from Hume, even beyond the point where his arguments were relevant to the American context.[18]

A decade of experience with themselves and the Articles of Confederation had disabused these American luminaries of any unwarranted optimism about their own abilities to stand aloof from self-interest that might have been generated during their remarkable revolution. As they drew themselves reluctantly back into the folds of Hume's philosophy, Madison's lament that men are not angels became again an American commonplace. That basic assumption about the nature of man or the expectations that we might have for human behavior lies at the very root of constitutionalist thought. For if men will not abuse power and are capable of error-free decision making, there is no need of a constitution. Madison certainly did not claim that every man would necessarily abuse power when given the opportunity. But, from a statistical point of view, he would say that any institution which permitted or rewarded the abuse of power would eventually degenerate into tyranny.

POLITICAL THEORY AND CONSTITUTIONALISM

The assumption of self-interest and abuse of power shapes constitutionalist thought at several levels. Whether articulated or not, it is the insight that compels all human societies to recognize that laws are essential for human interaction. Not only are men generally incapable of coming to a full agreement on general moral principles of conduct, but they are even less capable of consistently adhering to those principles once established. And so, law becomes necessary to make life in society tenable. Law becomes a substitute for that moral and intellectual ideal which the human imagination continually generates anew. Given the nature of man, law is the highest form of social organization to which we can in fact achieve.

At a second level, law requires enforcement and enforcement agencies. Governments with coercive power create a second level on which human selfishness and power lust can act out their course. Constitutionalist thinkers have recognized the necessity of institutional constraints on public authorities to prevent them from corrupting the rule of law. Legal rules limiting the officials are of no value if there are no institutional procedures and balancing arrangements that check them from corrupting the rules through arbitrary and self-interested interpretations.

For a society to maintain its laws over time, it must agree in advance on the procedures and officials by which future disputes under the law will be decided. The community must also determine how those officials will be selected at any point in time. These are constitutional choices. But the science of constitutionalism focuses most importantly on a third choice—the balancing of governmental institutions to prevent them from degenerating into perverse instruments for advancing the private fortunes of government officials or of some privileged class.

Francis Wormuth was one of the first to help contemporary scholars see that the essence of constitutionalism is this concern with "auxiliary precautions" as they were called by James Madison, or "contrivances which not only describe but confine government, at least in its everyday activities."[19] F. A. Hayek eventually came very close to this when he defined constitutional law as a superstructure erected to secure the maintenance of the law, rather than the source of all other law.[20] McIlwain was less sensitive to the problem of institutional devices in his definition of constitutionalism as "the limitation of government by law," although his studies of the English constitution clearly indicate that he saw the weakness of the English constitution in its failure to develop institutions which could balance the governing authority of the king over a period of four centuries.[21] Much less appreciation for this definition is evident in the writings of Tom Paine, for example, who saw constitutions as "antecedent to a government" and believed that governments were "only a creature of a constitution."[22]

Because constitutions set the conditions for lawmaking, it is commonly assumed that laws are somehow derivative from and subsequent to constitutions. But the opposite view is more easily defended from the historical record, which shows that law usually precedes a constitution. It is specifically to preserve the law and the regular administration of law that constitutions have been designed. The whole point of a constitution is to protect the law of the people which seems to be threatened by their rulers. The examples of the endless series of medieval charters such as the Magna Charta comes to mind where the people would rise up— not to overthrow the king—but to compel him to promise to maintain and respect the law or "the liberties of the people." History credits those wise conquerors who have preserved the law of the conquered nations. This was the wisdom of the Romans and the Norman invaders of Britain.

The least comprehending definition of constitutionalism is one that sees it as an exercise of moralistic political theory committed to the task of discovering the correct fundamental principles for reconciling liberty and equality. This latter moralistic enterprise has virtually consumed the attention of our political and legal philosophers today. Few of these are concerned to identify practical institutional devices that would prevent the kinds of inequities or violations of right on which they focus. Rather, their concern is to find some philosophical principle which defines just law from a moral point of view.

I do not question that this is an interesting and worthwhile enterprise. But to see its connection with reality, we must remember that legal and constitutional thought have to start from a recognition that people do not always act on the basis of disinterested moral principle. Our experience teaches us that they act from self-interest and that, before morality can become a guiding feature of social life, self-interest must be controlled in practical ways. We will not pave the way to Utopia by finally discovering the true philosophical account of justice. Rather, Utopia could only be possible in a world where men had ceased to pursue self-interest at the expense of others—where they had ceased to be men and had become angels.

Much of the contemporary failure to recognize institutional safeguards as the true basis of our freedoms stems from our uncritical acceptance of the claims of the moralistic enterprise. One European historian praises the French Declaration of the Rights of Man of 1789 specifically because it "is concerned with the rights of man, not the rights of the citizen." In other words, it focuses on "universal human rights," which focus will in time produce "the new man" and "the new citizen."[23] De Ruggiero gives us here a marvelous example of the naivete of the extreme liberal view that once people hear the moral truth, they will naturally conform their lives and social institutions to it. Where would the Americans be today if Madison had believed that?

It is not likely that we could find in the eighteenth century a document which reflects a stronger commitment to the principles of freedom under law than does the French Declaration of the Rights of Man. Yet the French Revolution failed to produce that freedom. My argument is that a significant part of the reason for that failure is that the announcement of true political principles in a constitution accomplishes nothing and may be counterproductive. For if the government is not properly designed and balanced to prevent the emergence of a tyrant, the principles will be interpreted by officials who are free to use the power of government to pursue their own ends, and the principles will be as nothing. James Madison repeatedly referred to constitutional articulations of general constitutional principles as "mere parchment barriers."[24] Certainly the Americans believed in most of the principles announced so confidently to the world by the French. But they mention none of them in their own Constitution. Upon reflection we can see in their work profound evidence of the genius and effectiveness of centuries of constitutional experience in England and colonial America. The Americans set their hands directly to the problem of designing an internal balance and complication of decision-making processes that would prevent the concentration of power in the hands of a single faction.

There is among English-speaking populations a simple rule for dividing a cake which epitomizes their constitutional wisdom. The rule does not say the cake must be divided evenly or that it should be divided on some other principle of fairness. The rule simply says, "He who cuts the cake must choose his piece last." This rule is no less concerned with equality and fairness than is the liberal French rhetoric. But without mentioning such principles it brings them far more effectively into reality.

No legal theorist has attracted more attention in the last twenty years than has Ronald Dworkin.[25] Yet Dworkin has publicly urged the Supreme Court and judges generally to see their responsibility to reach behind the law to the unquestionably true principle of equality to guide them in the resolution of difficult cases.[26] This dangerous course can only serve to provide rationalizations for those who would promote their own political and moral views through law and in the process create legal confusion and destroy our ability to predict the legal implications of our actions, as the rule of law requires.

And so I emphasize my conclusion that natural law, or any moralistic theory of constitutionalism, fails radically to see that the root of law is not moral truth. It is rather convention, agreement, which may or may not be derived from the popular morality, but it is emphatically not natural law. This may be a pessimistic view; but it is nonetheless true that it is the lot of men in communities to live by law as a substitute for moral truth.

To live by moral truth as a community seems beyond us. And as every primitive society and historical culture that has achieved freedom under a constitution has discovered, that freedom has come through institutional design and balance and not through philosophical or ethical discoveries.

The kind of attack that I have made on constitutional articulations of abstract rights or metalegal principles is easily misunderstood and may need clarification. In the first place I should stipulate that it is not an attack on the idea or the existence of rights. Rather, most constitutionalists do assume that people have rights. Furthermore, I strongly endorse moral philosophy as an important enterprise in helping us see the implications of different theories of rights. I believe that pro-rights propaganda efforts are a very positive contribution to political society and provide necessary encouragement for the maintenance and protection of those rights through constitutional devices.

However, on the basis of practical considerations, we must reject the abstract rights approach to constitutionalism. The constitutional problem is the practical problem of preventing public authorities from corrupting the law. It is the law which articulates our liberties or rights. Abstract statements of rights or constitutional principle are worthless in constitutions. My argument is based on the observation that only institutional balancing has any real effect. Furthermore, I would argue on the negative side that statements of abstract rights are potentially very mischievous, this because an unchecked authority can interpret such general statements of right to suit its own interest and then exploit the sweeping substantive language. The liberals who do not believe this should remind themselves of the substantive due process reasoning developed by conservative American judges near the end of the last century.

A further practical reason for avoiding the abstract rights approach is that it requires theoretical agreement on the content and justification of the rights protected. Political agreements on policies to be pursued or institutional devices to be used in decision making can be reached between parties which might never be able to reach agreement on their reasons or justifications for those policies, or their theories about rights. A moralistic approach to constitutions which seeks to preserve rights by incorporating abstract or principled articulations of rights in constitutional documents has far lower prospects for developing adequate popular support for any single theory to be adopted. We can agree much more quickly on institutional and policy statements than on theoretical ones.

My argument therefore is not against the enterprise of moralistic, political philosophy. This has an essential and positive function. The error of many moralistic philosophers lies in their uncritical jump from abstract moral thought to constitutional theorizing. I do not necessarily disagree with their moral views. But I believe they are too often naive about constitutions. They do not exhibit adequate understanding of constitutionalism.

The most frequent mistake of the moralistic philosophers in making that jump is the assumption of benevolence which sneaks in unnoticed. Rawls, for example, acknowledges that there will be strains placed on the contract from the poor, but he does not anticipate the strains which will come from the better off, who are being taxed to help the poor. The assumption of benevolence is not recognized or discussed. And this is characteristic of the moralistic approaches to constitutions, which overlook the problem of human nature at its crucial point of application.

The constitutional problem is a permanent feature of human society which can never, even in principle, be finally solved once and for all. There will never be one perfect institutional design which will solve the problem of tyranny forever. As described earlier, human nature is such that inventive men seeking their own interests will always find ways to work new angles and corrupt or undermine institutional arrangements which may have functioned successfully in the past. Natural or external events can also dramatically affect the artificial balances of a constitution as migrations bring cultural mixing, or as famines, wars, and plagues change the configuration of populations and the conditions of life. Economic growth has a similar effect. All of these can have constitutional consequences. Because constitutionalism addresses a permanent problem, it is essential that we pay attention to it in a systematic way and preserve the wisdom that the centuries have brought us for dealing with these changes.

Finally, all constitutionalist thought assumes that law is the appropriate response to the problems of human nature and community. The rule of law creates the context of freedom whereby individual men may pursue moral perfection as they understand it without inflicting their own views of perfection on others. Law is the means by which we prevent arbitrary or willful interventions in the lives of individuals by those who must necessarily be chosen to enforce the rules of the game.

PUBLIC VIRTUE AND CONSTITUTIONALISM

It could reasonably be argued that the beliefs of ordinary people influence the fortunes of constitutional government more than the theories of philosophers. A universal feature of successful constitutional regimes has been a cultural commitment to rule of law. For a constitution to succeed, the community belief systems must support its aims. There must be a commitment to the law and rule of law. "Constitutionalism means that all power rests on the understanding that it will be exercised according to commonly accepted principles."[27]

It is the absence of that cultural commitment among the people themselves which explains the ongoing failure of Latin American attempts to imitate the American Constitution. In too many countries, the oppressive culture of the strongman is ingrained in the people. Even when the peasants successfully revolt and come to power, they turn the tables and become themselves oppressors, not only of their vanquished predecessors but of their own class, in a cycle which has played itself out now for two centuries. Solzhenitsyn attributes the amazingly successful imposition of strong communist rule on a compliant Russian citizenry to a similar cultural defect.[28]

The eighteenth-century Americans, on the contrary, had the benefit of cultural expectations built up through centuries of English commitment to rule of law and constitutionalism. A century of benign neglect allowed them to develop de facto institutions for self-government as well as inflated views of what their legal rights as Englishmen might be. When the central government undertook to restore firm control over the colonies after 1760, it was too late. And when the newly independent Americans undertook to form a new government, they remembered that good government requires some private sacrifices. The Americans of the late eighteenth century enjoyed a unique heritage in that they understood the dependence of freedom upon rule of law and constitutional government, while they were also willing to make some personal sacrifices to establish and maintain a republican form of government. Most of their eighteenth- and nineteenth-century imitators were not so fortunate.

ANALYSIS OF RULE OF LAW

At mid-century it might well have seemed that serious interest in the idea of rule of law was almost dead among intellectuals. The concept had fallen into disuse, and the understanding of that concept was certainly in decline among legal and political philosophers. The ideology of democracy and equality had taken over center stage in the discussions of academicians. However, in 1960 F. A. Hayek published an analysis of rule of law that went beyond anything developed by earlier thinkers.[29] Since Hayek's book, other notable scholars have made further statements on the subject. In 1964 Lon Fuller identified certain principles, or norms, which constitute an "inner morality of law"—principles including generality, publicity, clarity, coherence, and possibility.[30] In 1966 J. R. Lucas published an important elaboration of the analysis of rule of law that was also partially derived from Hayek's discussion.[31] Finally, in 1975 John Rawls used the notion to bolster his process theory of justice, even though he treats the subject from a moralistic point of view.[32] In his 1980 book, John Finnis used the idea of law to try to bridge the classic gap between accounts of natural law and natural rights.[33] And in 1983 Michael Oakeshott published the essay which brings formal discussion of the issues to its highest level.[34] But most political and legal philosophers continue to ignore this issue and do not put much emphasis on an analysis of the concept.

Because the notion of rule of law is crucial for an understanding of constitutionalism, it is essential that we develop an adequate account of the concept. On the face of it, there are discrepancies of serious magnitude between the various accounts mentioned above and within each individual account. Even Hayek's groundbreaking account fails to make certain elementary and essential distinctions. The question then seems to be, how can we lay out the logical elements of the concept to provide some coherent order for its attendant principles, assumptions, and implications? The following paragraphs are only a summary of preliminary points that should be considered before taking on this larger creative project.

Any discussion of rule of law begins with the assumption that liberty is desirable, that there is a need to protect a sphere of individual freedom. That may be regarded as a moral value, but it may also be regarded as a simple preference. People want to have freedom for themselves. As we begin to answer the question of how that freedom might be obtained, we need to make a further assumption about the nature of the world in which we live, particularly the nature of man himself. What kind of a creature is it that we want to make free? This is not a metaphysical question. Rather it is an empirical inquiry which asks what tendencies we should expect to observe in human behavior.

There are several answers that might be given to this. We might, for example, assume that men are naturally cooperative and respectful of the rights of one another, in which case we would then conclude that some form of anarchy or possibly a moral utopia of some sort might be possible to achieve. If we assume, with the more conservative tradition in western thought, that men will generally pursue their own self-interest—even, in many cases, at the expense of innocent third parties—and that we cannot expect men to either know or discover the truth, then we will conclude that a society of law offers the best practical alternative political regime. On that view, laws would be the practical substitute for moral principles in a regime in which it is recognized that general adherence to true moral principles is not a rational expectation.

We can define the society of law, or the rule of law, as an arrangement in which the individual is able to plan his own life by adhering to rules by which he will avoid all penalties enforced by law. Such a definition entails several assumptions.

1. It assumes generality, that rules lay down general standards of conduct for all citizens equally.
2. It assumes that the rules will be stated with sufficient *clarity*, that there is little or no question what forms of behavior are permitted or prohibited by the rule.
3. It assumes that the rules are coherent, that is, that there is an established hierarchy to determine which rules govern in cases of conflict and that there are not conflicts in the rules governing the same situations.
4. It assumes that the rules are public, that they are available and known to the citizens.
5. It assumes that the rules are possible, that they can be followed, that they do not require impossible or even unreasonable behavior.
6. It assumes that the rules when created are prospective, that they refer to their own future and not to the past.
7. It assumes that the rules are backed by authoritative enforcement, that there is a governmental structure responsible for determining cases of conflict under the rules.

Once we have identified these necessary characteristics of the rules themselves, we can inquire into the characteristics of the institutions which might be expected to maintain and enforce this kind of rules without interjections of arbitrary will. Recognizing the natural institutional tendency toward tyranny inherent in our assumption about human nature, we could recommend that the government have the following general characteristics:

1. It should be based on a separation of powers. The power to make laws must be separated institutionally from the power to enforce the laws. This is fundamentally a restriction that legislators may not enforce their own rules.

2. Every individual must have equal legal rights as he confronts the enforcement of law.
3. The government must be subject to the periodic approval of the people it rules. The point is to prevent tyranny through responsible government. Consent should be achieved in two ways. There is assumed at a most fundamental level a constitutional agreement. The second level is the consent to officials who will decide on the laws and the enforcement of law. Republicanism was a modern theory of consent.
4. An independent judiciary seems to be necessary in principle to protect rule of law from potentially tyrannical governments.
5. Hayek has pointed out that there must always be provision for exceptions to any of the above principles or to laws that may be valid in a given polity. But in principle, such exceptions must be both justified and compensated at the time.

The principles listed above and others not mentioned seem to include rules which are enjoined on legislatures and judges. But the rules are not self-enforcing. There need to be institutional devices that will carry the rules into effect. The actual devices used in any particular political system might vary widely. Some devices will be more successful than others. But the rules themselves will often appear ambiguous in concrete situations. It is therefore necessary to institute procedural standards as the only effective way of enforcing the guidelines. As one examines the provisions of the American Constitution one is struck by the fact that none of the principles of rule of law are announced or explained, or even set forth. Rather, the document only lists the procedures and the devices by which the Founders hoped to achieve the effect of the principles identified here.

Many of these principles are implemented at least partially through specific prohibitions on the powers of government or specific institutional devices. For example, the principle of generality is supported by the prohibition on bills of attainder; the principle of prospectivity is implemented by the prohibition on ex post facto laws. Some of Fuller's principles such as clarity, coherence, and possibility, tend to be implemented primarily through judicial rules of interpretation. We find laws which are unconstitutionally vague to be unacceptable in our system. We have a supremacy clause which gives some hierarchy and coherence in the legal system as a means of supplementing judicial rules of interpretation. Publicity is protected by the prohibitions on the infringement of free press and speech as well as the requirement that legislatures publish their proceedings and that legislatures and courts deliberate in the public view.

The principle of separation of powers is implemented with a large collection of constitutional devices. Most notable among these are the division of the operation of government into three branches and the further division of the legislative branch into two parts. Institutions such as judicial review and the various checks and balances protect the independence and integrity of the three branches, thus indirectly supporting the notion of separation of powers. Madison called this the doctrine of partial agency.

Formal equality is implemented in specific provisions prohibiting creation of royalty and nobility as well as rules guaranteeing equal legal rights to citizens of every state. The principle of consent is primarily implemented through the mechanisms of representative government, as well as the provisions for the ratification of the Constitution and subsequent amendments. An independent judiciary is provided through prohibitions on juggling either the tenure or the salaries of judges during their service. Protection from exceptions occurs in the eminent domain clause.

SUMMARY

In this essay I have briefly looked at the political institutions of a wide variety of societies to demonstrate the universality of both the political problem (the tendency to tyranny) and the best human solution (rule of law under the protection of constitutional arrangements). As an antidote to the decline in our understanding and appreciation for the idea of rule of law I have argued that constitutions should be seen as collections of institutional devices or arrangements designed to prevent the emergence of tyrants in the process of settling private or public disputes, and not as pronouncements of general principles of political morality.

Secondly, I have insisted that not every collection of institutional devices will constitute an adequate constitution. To succeed, a constitution must preserve and promote the rule of law, the point of which is to make official response to private action as predictable and avoidable as possible for the citizen. No amount of moralizing or breast-beating will compensate for a well-conceived system that provides practical barriers to factional take-over of the powers of the state. And inappropriate reliance on moral principle as law can give factional interests the weapon they need to implement their despotic programs.

Finally, I have recognized that the possibility that any particular polity will be able to achieve and maintain a system of law depends as well on the extent to which the political culture includes a commitment to law as a means of creating that individual sphere of freedom to pursue the good. Rule of law, by refusing to nationalize moral truth, makes its universal pursuit at the individual and voluntary-association level a concrete possibility.

Notes

1. Walter H. Hamilton, "Constitutionalism," in *Encyclopedia of the Social Sciences*, vol. 4 (London: Macmillan, 1930–35), 255.

2. Ibid.

3. Lucy Mair, *Primitive Government* (Harmondsworth, England: Pelican, 1962).

4. I am grateful to Merlin G. Myers for sharing these observations based on his dissertation research.

5. Hilda Kuper, "The Swazi: A South African Kingdom," in *Case Studies in Cultural Anthropology*, ed. George and Louise Spindler (New York: Holt, Rhinehart and Winston, 1963).

6. Max Gluckman, *Rituals of Rebellion in South-East Africa* (Manchester: Manchester University Press, 1954).

7. See Noel B. Reynolds, "Plato's Defense of Rule of Law," in the forthcoming proceedings of the World Congress for the Philosophy of Law and Social Philosophy, Athens, 1985, where I defend this controversial claim about Plato. That Plato understood and defended the idea of rule of law as an appropriate ideal for human societies is evident in all the epistles and in almost all of the dialogues. The exception is *Republic*, which gives an ironic defense of philosophical totalitarianism, which many commentators have mistakenly taken at face value.

8. This comment was originally published in Jeremy Bentham, "Leading Principles of a Constitutional Code, for any State," *The Pamphleteer*, No. 44 (London, 1823), II, n. 7. It can now be found in John Bowring, ed., *The Works of Jeremy Bentham*, vol. 2 (Edinburgh: William Tait, 1843), 273.

9. See the excellent and very brief discussion in Harvey C. Mansfield, Jr., "Constitutionalism and the Rule of Law," *Harvard Journal of Law and Public Policy* 8 (1985): 323–26.

10. Pindar, *De Pindar: The Odes of Pindar, Including the Principal Fragments*, intro. and trans. Sir John Sandys, ed. T. E. Page, Loeb Classical Library (London: William Heineman, Ltd., 1946), 169. The Greek text reads, *"nomos ho panton basileus."*

11. Charles H. McIlwain, *The Growth of Political Thought in the West* (London: Macmillan, 1932), 3.

12. See Brian Tierney, *The Crisis of Church and State* (Englewood Cliffs, N.J.: Prentice-Hall, 1964).

13. Otto Gierke, *Political Theories of the Middle Age*, trans. F. W. Maitland (Cambridge: Cambridge University Press, 1900).

14. Charles H. McIlwain, *Constitutionalism, Ancient and Modern*, rev. ed. (Ithaca: Cornell University Press, 1947), 77–79.

15. Francis D. Wormuth, *The Origins of Modern Constitutionalism* (New York: Harper, 1949).

16. James Madison, *The Federalist*.

17. Frederick G. Whelan, *Order and Artifice in Hume's Political Philosophy* (Princeton: Princeton University Press, 1985), 348–73, is an excellent new study which thoroughly vindicates the eighteenth-century Americans' reading of Hume.

18. Garry Wills, *Explaining America* (New York: Doubleday, 1981).

19. Wormuth, *Origins of Modern Constitutionalism*, 3.

20. F. A. Hayek, *Law, Legislation, and Liberty* (Chicago: University of Chicago Press, 1976).

21. McIlwain, *Constitutionalism*, 21.

22. Ibid., 14.

23. Guido de Ruggiero, *History of European Liberalism*, trans. R. G. Collingwood (Oxford: Oxford University Press, 1927).

24. See *The Federalist*, Nos. 47–51.

25. Ronald M. Dworkin, *Taking Rights Seriously* (London: Duckworth, 1977).

26. Ronald M. Dworkin, *Political Judges and the Rule of Law* (London: The British Academy, 1980), 282.

27. F. A. Hayek, *The Constitution of Liberty* (Chicago: University of Chicago Press, 1960), 181.

28. See especially Aleksander Solzhenitsyn, *The Gulag Archipelago*, trans. H. T. Willetts, vol. 3 (New York: Harper and Row, 1978).

29. Hayek, *Constitution of Liberty*, 205–19.

30. Lon L. Fuller, *The Morality of Law*, rev. ed. (New Haven: Yale University Press, 1969), 33–94.

31. J. R. Lucas, *The Principles of Politics* (Oxford: Clarendon Press, 1966), 106–62.

32. John Rawls, *A Theory of Justice* (Cambridge: Harvard University Press, 1975), 235–43.

33. John Finnis, *Natural Law and Natural Rights* (New York: Oxford University Press, 1980), 266–90.

34. Michael Oakeshott, "The Rule of Law," in *On History* (Oxford: Basil Blackwell, 1983), 119–64.

V

CIVIC VIRTUE: THE FOUNDERS' CONCEPTION AND THE TRADITIONAL CONCEPTION

★

Thomas L. Pangle

My purpose in this essay is to resuscitate serious discussion of a theme that was paramount at the time of the American Founding but that has since receded from public discourse. Today, talk of virtue tends to sound at best archaic; and when we are reminded that Americans of every rank and station were once prone to speak of politics in terms of virtue, we are likely to suppose that they did so for the sake of rhetorical ornamentation or—insofar as they were deadly serious—that their speech was the rather thoughtless expression of the peculiar moral prejudices of the times. While there is some truth to this impression, it by no means conveys the whole truth. If we look to the few most thoughtful or perspicacious of the influential Founders, we find that they usually refer to virtue with a gravity or care that indicates the weight they attach to the theme—but also the somewhat

---

Thomas Pangle is a Professor of Political Science at the University of Toronto.

puzzling or uneasy position the notion has come to assume in their thought. I wish to show that by rediscovering, reenacting for ourselves, and extending the Founders' incomplete but probing reflection on virtue, we can begin to take part in an unaccustomed but fruitful meditation on the requirements of sound republican life not only in the founding era but in all times and places.

Let us first recall several of the most emphatic of the leading Founders' appeals to the idea that the new Constitution depended on a special kind and degree of civic spirit among both leaders and citizenry. In the *Federalist,* Hamilton and Jay open their defense of the new Constitution by calling for a reinvigoration of the moral qualities displayed during the Revolution: a genuine sense of fraternity, a capacity for individual self-sacrifice, and and a dedication to "the noble enthusiasm of liberty": "one united people . . . who, by their joint counsels, arms, and efforts, fighting side by side throughout a long and bloody war, have nobly established their general liberty . . . a band of brethren, united to each other by the strongest ties" (1:35, 2:38). The work moves to its conclusion with Hamilton declaring that "the only solid basis of all our rights" is "public opinion, and . . . the general spirit of the people and of the government" (84:514–15). Madison spoke in a more purely classical vein when he rose on June 20, 1788, to defend the new Constitution in the debates at the Virginia Ratifying Convention: "I go on this great republican principle, that the people will have virtue and intelligence to select men of virtue and wisdom. Is there no virtue among us? To suppose that any form of government will secure liberty or happiness without any virtue in the people is a chimerical idea" (cf. *Federalist* 55:346). Ten days earlier, in the same debates, John Marshall spoke of "certain fundamental principles, from which a free people ought never to depart." These included "the favorite maxims of democracy: A strict observance of justice and public faith, and a steady adherence to virtue."[1]

These appeals to "favorite maxims of democracy" and a "great republican principle" are only two of many signs that the Founders thought of themselves as in some measure the heirs to a *tradition* of republican reflection on virtue, a tradition originating in Greco-Roman antiquity. Testimony to this legacy is seen in the pen name the authors of the *Federalist* chose: "Publius"—a name intended (as Madison later remarked in his letter to Paulding of July 23, 1818) to evoke Plutarch's biography of the heroic founder of the Roman republic, Publius Valerius Publicola. (Hamilton had used the same pen name nine years before, and it can be argued that he, especially, took it very seriously).[2] Such evocations of classical republican heroism and public spirit were a salient feature of the rhetorical landscape during the founding debates, and they had a resonance that was more than merely decorative. This becomes especially evident if one looks beyond the *Federalist* to the lesser pamphlets and journal articles which supported ratification. There were, to be sure, striking exceptions. Noah Webster dared to proclaim that "virtue, patriotism, or love of country, never was and never will be, till men's natures are changed, a fixed, permanent principle and support of government."[3] Nevertheless, as the late Herbert J. Storing concluded in his compendious study of this and other lesser Federalist writings, "the typical Federalist was likely to look to the traditional principles of civic education and character-molding. . . . Teaching, and even preaching, are important for the Federalists, more important than a reading of *The Federalist* would suggest."[4]

Yet one must immediately add that, among the most thoughtful of the Federalists, such expressions of kinship with, and gratitude for, the classical or Roman tradition of republicanism are tempered by sharp criticism and a proud assertion of innovation. The *Federalist* begins with Publius declaring his receptivity to the frequently voiced opinion that "it seems to have been reserved to the people of this country . . . to decide . . . whether societies of men are really capable or not of establishing good government from reflection and choice, or whether they are forever destined to depend for their political constitutions on accident and force" (1:33). The constitutions of the original Publius, of Lycurgus, Solon, and even of Moses, do not seem, then, to have decided the question. Hamilton thus foreshadows the view he will state even more emphatically in *Federalist* No. 9:

> It is impossible to read the history of the petty republics of
> Greece and Italy without feeling sensations of horror and disgust
> at the distractions with which they were continually agi-
> tated, . . . If momentary rays of glory break forth from the

gloom, while they dazzle us with a transient and fleeting bril-
liancy, they at the same time admonish us to lament that the
vices of government should pervert the direction and tarnish the
luster of those bright talents and exalted endowments for which
the favored soils that produced them have been so justly celebrated. (71–72)

Hamilton stresses that there have been in history "a few glorious
instances" that stand as exceptions to the general past experience
of republicanism. But he goes on to confess that "if it had been
found impracticable to have devised models of a more perfect
structure, the enlightened friends to liberty would have been
obliged to abandon the cause of that species of government
[namely, 'republican government'] as indefensible" (9:72). In
other words, genuinely monarchic government, when properly
designed, is clearly superior to any form of republican government that has yet been known.

That Publius should view the republican tradition in such a
light ought not to surprise us when we remember that the authors
of the *Federalist*, like all of their brethren, were deeply influenced
by Locke, Hume, Smith, and, above all, Montesquieu. These
philosophers, especially Montesquieu, had undertaken a search-
ing and highly critical analysis of classical republicanism, focusing on the civic virtue that was the heart of that republicanism.
The *Spirit of the Laws* elaborates a detailed and comprehensive new
account of virtue, self-consciously opposed to the account offered
by the classical political philosophers, and intended in the final
analysis to reveal the unnatural character of republics grounded on
virtue.[5] It is difficult to say how deeply or clearly Montesquieu's
subtle teaching had penetrated the minds of even the most intelli-
gent American readers. What is certain is that in the pages of the
Federalist we find many of the key features of the Montesquieuian
critique, stated in a more polemical tone reminiscent of Hume.
Guided by Montesquieu and Hume, we may order and summarize the *Federalist*'s version of the argument as follows.

The civic heroism exhibited by the ancient citizens and por-
trayed by their historians arose from and remained entrenched in
an unwise zeal for direct political self-determination, a zeal associated with small, tightly packed, urban societies. The diminutive
size of these civic republics left them prey to the unceasing danger

of foreign invasion, while their fierce and jealous sense of independence rendered them incapable of concerted defense (4:48–49;
18:passim). Thus exposed, they naturally tended to transform
their citizens into soldiers, their cities into armed camps; but
instead of achieving security by such measures, they succeeded
only in spawning imperialistic capacities and longings (6:53–57).
This waspish militarism was a principal source of the pressure
towards conformity or homogeneity that exerted itself relentlessly
on domestic politics within the classical republic. There were
other sources, however, which had even greater significance.

Chief among these was the attempt to stifle the internecine
factions endemic to the small city-republic by imbuing all citizens with similar tastes, opinions, and property holdings. This
effort inevitably failed, because it violated the natural diversity in
opinions, interests, and, above all, "in the faculties of men, from
which the rights of property originate"—a diversity which, being
rooted in man's fixed nature, cannot be removed or overcome for
long (10:78–79). What resulted from the doomed attempt, in
practice, was either the tyrannizing of the many by the few or,
more frequently in the long run, the tyranny of the majority—led
by some "heroic" demagogue (10:78–81; 63:389). "Most of the
popular governments of antiquity were of the democratic species," that is, regimes where "the people meet and exercise the
government in person" (14:100). But "in all very numerous assem-
blies, of whatever characters composed, passion never fails to
wrest the scepter from reason. Had every Athenian citizen been a
Socrates, every Athenian assembly would still have been a mob"
(55:342). The politics of such governments were tempestuous,
imprudent, and petty, endangering the security of every minority
and indeed of every single individual: "popular liberty" decreed
"to the same citizens the hemlock on one day and statues on the
next" (68:384). At the same time, the unchecked enthusiasm for
republican liberty tended to its own destruction through the
undermining of sound administration: because the assembly frequently sensed its own incapacity to carry on public administration, it was easily duped by demagogues or induced to surrender
itself to talented politicians and generals like Pericles (6:54–55;
10:79; 58:360). Even worse, the ancient city often found itself
compelled, on account of administrative crises, to have recourse
to absolute dictatorship (70:423–30). Those who sought domin-

ion of this kind were able to exploit the pervasive "superstition of the times, one of the principal engines by which government was then maintained" (18:123–24; 38:233).

This trenchant criticism—a criticism foreshadowed, in abbreviated form, by Jefferson in his attack on the Roman republic in *Notes on the State of Virginia* (Query 13)—all but compels the independent-minded reader to turn back to the classical historians and political theorists in order to judge the truth of Publius's charges, as well as to see more clearly just what the alternative notion of republicanism is against which the American version defines itself. For the thought of the *Federalist,* especially as regards virtue, represents neither a mere continuation nor a simple break with the tradition of classical republicanism.

When we do look back to the classical historians (e.g., Thucydides and Plutarch) and political theorists (e.g., Xenophon, Plato, Aristotle, and Cicero), we see that the *Federalist*'s characterization of ancient republicanism rings true in at least two massive respects. In contrast to the American Framers, classical republicanism tends to place much less weight on the need to secure individuals and their private liberties or "rights"—rights to private and familial preservation, to property, to freedom of religion, and to the "pursuit of happiness." Closely connected is the second great point of difference. The classics tend to attach more significance to republican self-government as an *end* or as a goal, and not simply a means to the protection of individual security. Yet, to focus as the *Federalist* tends to do on these two admittedly important contrasts is to run the risk of distorting seriously the nature of classical republicanism and that tradition's appeal to virtue. Such a distortion is indeed present in the *Federalist*'s presentation of the classical heritage, and if *we* are to gain a clear view of what is new and distinctive in the American conception of virtue, we must first try to see the classical tradition in its own terms.

To do so we must first draw a distinction between classical political practice (the actual conduct of affairs in republics like Sparta, Athens, and Rome) and classical political theory (the historians' and philosophers' critical reflections on this practice of the ancient cities). The classical political theorists are in their own way almost as severe (if more muted) in their criticism of the ancient city as are the authors of the *Federalist*.[6] But their criticism emerges out of a very different perspective. The classical theorists claim to articulate, to extend or apply, the city's *own* aspirations—the unfulfilled standards and goals present, even if only dimly, in the avowed principles of the most respectable civic factions. Those aspirations reveal, it is argued, that liberty or self-government, fraternity, and glory must be ranked *below* virtue—virtue conceived not as simply "civic" virtue, let alone as simply a necessary means to self-government.[7]

What does the classical tradition tend to mean by "virtue," and how and why does it assign to virtue, so understood, the highest priority among political goals? The classical analysis of virtue begins by giving full weight to the fact that the goals of politics which first come to sight as lending dignity to men are *freedom,* for one's own people, and *empire,* or rule, over other peoples; but the classics contend that reflection on the experience of freedom, and empire, reveals that these gleaming objects of ambition collapse into negative self-assertion and a vulgar or even slavishly dependent quest for prestige unless they are given more precise definition and limitation in terms of the virtues. The *virtues* are those rare qualities of character, seldom fully realized, through which human beings express in a graceful, orderly way their natural passions in coordination with intelligence. The four "cardinal" virtues are courage (the capacity to face fear of death on the battlefield, and lesser dangers in less urgent circumstances), moderation or temperance (the proper subordination of sensual appetite and pleasure), justice (reverence for law, unselfish and fair sharing, public spirit), and practical wisdom—exhibited especially in the supervisory or paternal care of inferiors. These qualities are valued in large part because they contribute to making society secure, prosperous, and free; but they are truly esteemed because they are not merely "good" (useful) but also partake of the "noble" or "beautiful" (in Greek, *to kalon*). According to the observations of the classical thinkers, the virtues cannot continue to flourish once they are valued only as means. The virtues, and virtuous men, cannot be adequately understood as instruments for liberty or for the release from danger and necessity; on the contrary, liberty, as something of inherent worth, only makes sense in the final analysis when it is seen as a means to, as an opportunity for the expression of, the virtues and virtuous men.

This becomes especially clear when one's gaze ascends from the sturdy virtues of the good soldier or citizen to the rare qualities of heart and mind possessed by the great leader and statesman. Here are found the strongest temptations and sternest challenges; here, above all, are the lawgivers like Lycurgus or Publius, who accept the awesome responsibility for laying down the fundamental principles, the distinguishing way of life, of an entire people for generations. To explore as well as to celebrate the characters of such men is the high function of the political historian like Plutarch or Tacitus. It is also the vocation of the artists: in the classical understanding, the virtues are the central focus of the fine arts, and the arts play a crucial role in politics, as the place for public inquiry into, judgment of, and education in the virtues. Through the portrayals of the artists, virtue comes to shining sight as constituting the perfection and hence the end or goal of humanity—as the full development of the most choiceworthy and admirable or excellent human qualities.

Now to the extent that the nobility or beauty of the virtues, in this comprehensive sense, comes to the fore, it becomes increasingly evident that "civic" virtue or "political" virtue (*aretē politikē*) points beyond itself to a fuller or more encompassing catalog of fulfilling human qualities. One of the most striking or unsettling features of classical republicanism, at least as it finds expression in the classical political theorists, is the extent to which "civic" virtue is treated as an incomplete or even somewhat deficient form of virtue. This tendency is most visible in Aristotle's *Ethics*,[8] and Plato's *Republic*[9] and *Laws*.[10] For the classics, it may be said, the virtues of the good citizen and statesman bulk large in, but surely do not exhaust, the virtues to which a good society aspires or which it seeks to foster. The excellences of the citizen as citizen, and even the virtues of most statesmen, are still largely the excellences of the good team member or good team leader, who tends to see the team or community as higher in dignity than himself and his virtues, and whose behavior may be governed very much by inherited opinion, love of reputation, and shame—rather than by reason, love of the noble, and autonomous habit. The citizen as citizen is limited to activities which are in the main social or group endeavors. But man is not, at his highest, an exclusively political or social animal.

It was Aristotle who first gave the name "moral virtue" to the excellence that encompasses but surpasses civic virtue. The man of true moral virtue, the "perfect gentleman," is a man possessed of "greatness of soul." As such, his dedication to the cardinal virtues is animated by the conviction that he and his virtues do not exist for the sake of the city but rather the city exists for the sake of virtues, and a way of life, such as his. He welcomes and enjoys the challenges of civic life and honors bestowed by his fellow citizens, but he looks down on even the highest of such challenges and honors as ultimately ancillary to his virtue, which he prizes for its own sake more than for any of its specific accomplishments or rewards (including fame). An Aristotelian understanding of the morally virtuous man claims to bridge or at least narrow greatly the enormous gap Montesquieu finds between the principle of "honor" and the principle of "virtue."[11] If anything, Aristotle's man of greatness of soul is closer to Montesquieu's man of "honor" than to Montesquieu's man of "virtue."[12] Moral virtue as articulated by Aristotle reaches beyond courage and moderation, and does so not only with a view to justice and a lawgiver's or king's practical wisdom, but also to more private excellences such as generosity, "magnificent" artistic taste, wit, truthful conversation, and intimate friendship. As a consequence, the virtue of justice in the full sense becomes the great lawgiver's characteristic determination to foster, by legal sanction and political action, the widest possible education or habituation in all these virtues.

A long commentary could easily be written elucidating the nature of each of these moral virtues that good laws should enforce, but let us briefly consider only the virtue of truthfulness. At first sight, this virtue seems mainly a challenge to character rather than to understanding. It would seem that even children, if properly bred and inspired, could begin to partake of this excellence to a considerable extent. When, however, Aristotle presents his account of truthfulness, he opposes it to the vices of irony and boastfulness, and alludes to Socrates, who, he notes, while guilty of irony, for this very reason stands at the opposite pole from the boaster. We are thus stirred to a fuller reflection. We all realize of course how grotesque the boaster is, and how important it is for us to avoid appearing to be boasters. Yet if we reflect a bit, it dawns on us that in a subtle but deep sense everyone who claims to know what he does not truly know convicts himself of boasting. Such boasting is not only ignoble; it obscures from the boaster his true neediness, and hence his true good. The virtue of candor or honesty in public and private affairs thus leads, on deeper analysis, to a virtue or awareness of need that calls for very considerable inquiry and self-examination, and may even compel a fundamental reorientation of one's entire life—as the example of Socrates so vividly testifies.

This reflection helps us to begin to understand the movement of thought that leads moral virtue, at its summit, to look beyond the sphere of moral action altogether, toward the truly self-conscious life of intellectual virtue or contemplation, and toward the realm of the divine which is either the object of the contemplative life or the source of its most troubling challenges. It is this last step—the strict subordination of the human to the divine, and of action to thought, or the ranking of the statesman's life beneath that of the unstatesmanlike life of the philosopher—that marks most distinctly the authentic classical tradition of political philosophy and its conception of virtue. And yet this last step, the classical theorists insist, can be traced directly and clearly to the deepest concerns of even the simplest citizen: the need to be truthful and to be in the right, above all when it comes to divine law and divine retribution.

It was this transpolitical culmination of the classic conception of virtue that was largely responsible for making possible an eventual assimilation of the classic moral heritage by the Christian tradition. Thomas Aquinas's synthesis of Aristotelian political philosophy and the New Testament remained authoritative throughout the Anglican Communion by virtue of Richard Hooker's *Laws of Ecclesiastical Polity,* the influence of which is evident in James Wilson's Lectures on Law of 1790–91. Space does not permit a detailed account of the important modifications the classical conception of civic and moral virtue had to undergo in order to become compatible with the principles of the Sermon on the Mount. It must suffice to note that not only were the theological virtues of faith, hope, and charity added to the canon of cardinal virtues, but, in addition, the idea of a "Christian gentleman" was colored by a new stress on human sinfulness, on the propriety of humility, on the suprapolitical authority of priests, and on disdain for worldly ambition and pleasure. There remained within that idea considerable tension between its two components or roots. This tension was often exploited by the early modern political philosophers, like Locke, Montesquieu, and Hume, who sought to replace both the Christian and the classical ideals—and who so strongly influenced the American Founders. But neither their rhetorical exaggerations nor their well-taken observations should obscure the massive common ground shared by the classical and Christian traditions, in contrast to the notion of virtue we find emerging in the modern period, and in particular among the Founders.

Once we have brought into view even a bare outline of what the classical tradition meant by "virtue" (in its original form or as modified by Christian political theology), we begin to realize the extent to which there lies at the heart of the American version of republicanism a *new* understanding of both the nature and the status of virtue. One approaches the core of the difference when one notes that the authors of the *Federalist,* like Jefferson,[13] tend to treat virtue (or piety) as at most an important *instrument* for security or ease, liberty, and fame. James Wilson seems to mark an important exception, for Wilson discovers in man's nature a "moral sense" which, in sharp contrast to Jefferson's conception of the "moral sense," is "totally distinct from the ideas of utility and agreeableness," and nonetheless "intended to regulate and control all our other powers." This "conscience" makes us "feel the beauty and excellence of virtue"; it reveals to us that "virtue and vice are ends, and are hateful or desirable on their own account." But as regards the realm where the virtues flourish, the same Wilson, addressing himself to women, taught that "publick government and publick law . . . were not made for themselves: they were made for something better; and of that something better, you form the better part—I mean society—I mean particularly domestick society. . . . in the just order of things, government is the scaffolding of society: and if society could be built and kept entire without government, the scaffolding might be thrown down, *without the least inconvenience or cause of regret"* (emphasis added).[14]

Jefferson, Publius, and Wilson could not have subordinated the virtues of public life to liberty, or pleasure, or fame, or the satisfactions and virtues of domesticity, without endorsing, simultaneously, a change in the meaning of virtue. Generally speaking, one may say that the *Federalist,* like the writings of Jefferson and other leading figures of the founding generation, deemphasizes the aristocratic pride or high-mindedness, the love of manly beauty, the reverence (including reverence for one's own soul), and the austere or Stoic self-restraint which bulked so large in the classical image of the virtuous gentleman.[15] The old cardinal virtues are still honored: but they are infused with a new spirit and expressed in new practices, and thereby change decisively their nature.

While the authors of the *Federalist* make no reference to the "moral sense," in the manner of Wilson or even in the manner of Jefferson, they do not ignore the "conscience" and even close by appealing to it (85:522; cf. 81:488). However, Jay characteristically links it to "reputation" rather than to divine sanction (64:396). On the whole, the *Federalist* remains almost totally silent about awe for the divine, and respect for the contemplative life that claims to be closest to the divine. Publius does, it is true, lay faint claim to divine assistance in the creation of the Constitution: "It is impossible for the man of pious reflection not to perceive in it a finger of that Almighty hand which has been so frequently and signally extended to our relief in the critical stages of the revolution" (37:230–31). But, mindful above all of the threat of religious persecution and the horrors of religious warfare, the Founders scrupulously refrain from claiming any divine inspiration or from suggesting any important connection between the Constitution and any specific conception of piety or of divinity. They agree, it would seem, with John Adams's earlier assessment of the role Americans assigned to divinity in the making of their constitutions:

> It was the general opinion of ancient nations that the Divinity alone was adequate to the important office of giving laws to men . . .
>
> The United States of America have exhibited, perhaps, the first example of governments erected on the simple principles of nature; and if men are now sufficiently enlightened to disabuse themselves of artifice, imposture, hypocrisy, and superstition, they will consider this event as an era in their history. . . . It will never be pretended that any persons employed in [framing the several governments of the states] had interviews with the gods or were in any degree under the inspiration of Heaven, more than those at work upon ships or houses, or laboring in merchandise or agriculture; it will forever be acknowledged that

116

these governments were contrived merely by the use of reason and the senses . . . Neither the people nor their conventions, committees, or subcommittees considered legislation in any other light than as ordinary arts and sciences, only more important. . . . even the pious mystery of holy oil had no more influence than that other one of holy water. The people were universally too enlightened to be imposed on by artifice; . . . governments thus founded on the natural authority of the people alone, without a pretense of miracle or mystery, and which are destined to spread over the northern part of that whole quarter of the globe, are a great point gained in favor of the rights of mankind. [16]

This is not to deny that the Massachusetts Constitution of 1780 (authored by John Adams, along with Samuel Adams, John Hancock, and other Massachusetts luminaries) included in Articles Two and Three of its Declaration of Rights "the right as well as the duty of all men in society, publicly, and at stated seasons, to worship the SUPREME BEING"—and therefore instituted "the public worship of GOD" and "public instructions in piety, religion and morality" led by "public protestant teachers of piety, religion and morality," enjoining "upon all subjects an attendance upon the instructions of the public teachers aforesaid." In other words, we must not forget that there indeed persisted, especially at lower levels of government in the founding period, strong embers of the classical and Christian heritages. Yet, it must also be observed that it was these passages in the Massachusetts Constitution that occasioned the greatest debate at the convention, and the most controversy during adoption—in part because they were intermingled with other passages that seemed at odds with them. As Oscar and Mary Handlin sum up the situation, "Article III therefore was not so much the articulation of a theory as the description of such compromises, shaped by experience, as would be 'likely to hit the taste of the public.' " (This was a public, we may add, that was less consistent or rigorous or farsighted than were statesmen like Jefferson and the authors of the *Federalist*.)[17]

The displacement of religion and of even diluted versions of the purely intellectual or contemplative virtues from the public, political sphere to the private or "social" sphere goes hand in hand with the kindred displacement of the fine arts, especially poetry, and the moral virtues of appreciation for and patronage of the arts. In his presentation of the model lawgiver, Plutarch tells us that in Lycurgus' polity, "poetry and music were no less culti-vated than a concise dignity of expression." It is this, he says, that explains the remarkable fact that the kings of Sparta before every great battle always offered a public sacrifice to the goddesses of music—"putting their troops in mind of their education."[18] A not altogether untypical distant echo of this spirit is again to be found in the Massachusetts Constitution of 1780. In chapter 5, section 1, strong official provision is made for Harvard University on the ground that

> our wise and pious ancestors . . . laid the foundation of
> Harvard-College, in which University many persons of great emi-
> nence have, by the blessing of GOD, been initiated in those arts
> and sciences, which qualified them for public employments,
> both in Church and State: And whereas the encouragement of
> Arts and Sciences, and all good literature, tends to the honor of
> GOD, the advantage of the christian religion, and the great bene-
> fit of this, and the other United States of America.

Section two adds that

> wisdom, and knowledge, as well as virtue, diffused generally
> among the body of the people, being necessary for the preserva-
> tion of their rights and liberties . . . it shall be the duty of
> legislators and magistrates . . . to cherish the interests of lit-
> erature and the sciences . . . to encourage . . . rewards and
> immunities, for the promotion of agriculture, arts, sciences, com-
> merce, trades, manufactures, and a natural history of the coun-
> try; to countenance and inculcate the principles of humanity and
> general benevolence, public and private charity, industry and fru-
> gality, honesty and punctuality in their dealings; sincerity, good
> humour, and all social affections, and generous sentiments
> among the people.

The strongly utilitarian note that marks even this passage pre-pares us for the almost strictly prosaic concern with science that we find in the Constitution—despite the more liberal note envis-aged at one time during the Convention.[19] "To promote the Progress of Science and useful Arts" Congress is given the power to secure "for limited Times to Authors and Inventors the exclusive Right to their respective Writings and Discoveries."[20] The motives of charity or generosity, of pure passion for the truth or of love for that which is beautiful but useless, are neither celebrated nor particularly encouraged by this crucial constitutional linchpin of the technological and commercial society.

For the Constitution is intended to establish a "commercial republic" of unprecedented intensity, and the implications for the moral character of the inhabitants are profound and manifold.[21] Publius is well aware that some of the ancient republics were also "commercial" in character (6:57); but he stresses that among "modern" peoples, and especially among Americans, the "spirit of commerce" has attained an "unequalled" or even "unbridled" dynamism which renders the new American idea of a "commercial republic" qualitatively different from all earlier versions.

> The prosperity of commerce is now perceived and acknowledged by all enlightened statesmen to be the most useful as well as the most productive source of national wealth, and has accordingly become a primary object of their political cares. By multiplying the means of gratification, by promoting the introduction and circulation of the precious metals, those darling objects of human avarice and enterprise, it serves to vivify and invigorate all the channels of industry and to make them flow with greater activity and copiousness. The assiduous merchant, the laborious husbandman, the active mechanic, and the industrious manufacturer—all orders of men look forward with eager expectation and growing alacrity to this pleasing reward of their toils. (12:91)

From this we can begin to understand the new meaning of "moderation." The *Federalist* does indeed remark repeatedly on the value of this cardinal virtue: but what the new Publius means by this is much closer to the famous new interpretation offered by Montesquieu, and by his students or admirers Hume and Smith, than it is to any classical conception. What is praised is not so much a divine or noble and graceful coordination of appetite with reason for its own sake, but rather the enlightened, calm, and prudent pursuit of security and ease for oneself and for the society at large in which one finds oneself. Such moderation in no way excludes—in fact it promotes—a softness of manners and morals:

the vice which *this* version of moderation opposes is not material or sensual self-indulgence so much as fanaticism, including the religious and stoic or ascetic fanaticisms of past ages.[22]

It is this same moderation, or enlightened and sober self-interest, that the new Publius counts on as the root of the citizenry's respect for the law and devotion to or sense of justice. When Publius speaks (as he often does) of the "public good," or the "common good," and of justice, he generally seems to have in mind, apart from defense, the commercial prosperity of America as a whole, and the protection of individual rights, especially rights to the use of the "different and unequal faculties of acquiring property" (10:78).[23] The *Federalist* certainly does not disdain, but neither does it rely heavily upon, a sense of civic solidarity, deference for superiors (in age or virtue or knowledge), or traditional reverence for law. It is true that in this last key respect the authors of the *Federalist* depart less radically from the classical tradition than does Jefferson: the sole point on which Publius explicitly takes issue with Jefferson and his *Notes on the State of Virginia* is in regard to the evaluation of "reverence for the laws" (49:313–17).[24]

But, as we saw at the outset, *liberty* is the theme which elicits from the authors of the *Federalist* sentiments that hark back most powerfully to the classics. If the Founding Fathers do not look to virtue as the end of free government, they do treat love of liberty itself as an end and even as a kind of virtue. James Wilson, introducing in 1790 his famous course of lectures, with George Washington and John Adams in the audience, affirms:

When some future Xenophon or Thucydides shall arise to do justice to their virtues and all their actions; the glory of America will rival—it will outshine—the glory of Greece.

Were I called upon for my reasons why I deem so highly of the American Character, I would assign them in a very few words—that character has been eminently distinguished by the love of liberty, and the love of law . . .

Illustrious examples are displayed to our view, that we may imitate as well as admire. Before we can be distinguished by the same honors, we must be distinguished by the same virtues.

What are those virtues? They are chiefly the same virtues, which we have already seen to be descriptive of the American character—the love of liberty, and the love of law . . . Without liberty, law loses its nature and its name, and becomes oppression. Without law, liberty also loses its nature and its name, and becomes licentiousness. [25]

Directly connected is the high place that continues to be assigned to courage, as manifested on the battlefields of the Revolution, but also in the form of a proud spirit ready to assert its rights in peacetime. "What is to restrain the House of Representatives from making legal discriminations in favor of themselves and a particular class of the society?" Madison asks, and then answers: ". . . above all, the vigilant and manly spirit which actuates the people of America" (57:353). [26] Yet, as this very quotation suggests, American "manliness" is at least as intimately tied to vigilant self-interest as it is to vigilant public interest; it would be better to say that the hope or intention is to awaken the public interest by way of what Tocqueville was to call "self-interest rightly understood." Such a scheme can be expected to work only if Americans are seldom called upon to sacrifice themselves for the public good. Accordingly, Publius makes it clear that he hopes a strong union will make war less and less likely. Moreover, Publius shows that he hopes and expects that, for the mass of the citizens, intense involvement in politics will be rare, and aimed at rather temporary and restricted goals. Madison speaks with genuine gravity of "that honorable determination which animates every votary of freedom to rest all our political experiments on the capacity of mankind for self-government" (39:240). But he also locates the distinctive superiority of the American over all previous republics in the American system's use of *representative* government over a large nation—thereby making possible *"the total exclusion of the people in their collective capacity, from any share in"* governing (63:387, emphasis Madison's). The vast majority of citizens will participate only occasionally and mostly indirectly, through elections and jury duty. In exercising their electoral capacity, the people will display, to use Epstein's insightful formulation, "partisanship" rather than political "ambition." [27] They will characteristically act so as to support various partisan "factions" rooted for the most part in competing economic interests.

The energy and zeal the Founders seem to hope will characterize the new citizen, in a regime that protects true opportunity for each man's exercise of his faculties, is the sort of industry for which Benjamin Franklin, in his *Autobiography,* sought consciously to provide a vivid model. At the core of such a citizen is the ambition, ever restless but restricted in scope, of the frugal and temperate "self-made" man—a man who prudently discerns the link between his rise and the promotion of useful "projects" which benefit his neighbors and attract their esteem, affection, and assistance.[28] American "manliness," then, manifests itself most naturally and readily not in battles but in "adventurous" entrepreneurship "which distinguishes the commercial character of America," and "has already excited uneasy sensations in . . . Europe" (11:85): "the industrious habits of the people of the present day, absorbed in the pursuits of gain and devoted to the improvements of agriculture and commerce, are incompatible with the condition of a nation of soldiers, which was the true condition of the people of those [ancient] republics" (8:69).[29]

The *Federalist* here echoes, with some mitigation, the more blunt judgment of David Hume: "But as these principles [of ancient virtue] are too disinterested, and too difficult to support, it is requisite to govern men by other passions, and animate them with a spirit of avarice and industry, art and luxury." As Ralph Lerner remarks, "American commercial republicans did not promote this new policy with quite the breezy equanimity of Hume." But, "neither did the leading Americans reject Hume's premises."[30] Even the Antifederalists, who oppose the Constitution in part in the name of a more virtuous vision of society, are practically unanimous in their commitment to a commercial society and an economy of growth.[31] Thomas Jefferson voices more strongly than any other Federalist the kind of fear Tocqueville was later to substantiate and make more precise with his notions of "individualism" and "tyranny of the majority"; the fear that Americans would more and more exhibit a syndrome of apathetic withdrawal into narrow economic interests and petty personal spheres, their basely egalitarian spirits deformed and dwarfed by an inner dependence on amorphous, mass "public opinion." To forestall or slow such development, Jefferson insists, in celebrated passages in the *Notes on the State of Virginia,* on the intimate link between true virtue and the unique sort of economic and personal independence farming seems to foster:

Those who labour in the earth are the chosen people of God, if ever he had a chosen people, whose breasts he has made his peculiar deposit for substantial and genuine virtue. . . . Corruption of morals in the mass of cultivators is a phenomenon of which no age nor nation has furnished an example. It is the mark set on those, who not looking up to heaven, to their own soil and industry, as does the husbandman, for their subsistence, depend for it on the casualties and caprice of customers. Dependence begets subservience and venality, suffocates the germ of virtue, and prepares fit tools for the designs of ambition. This, the natural progress and consequence of the arts, has sometimes perhaps been retarded by accidental circumstances: but, generally speaking, the proportion which the aggregate of the other classes of citizens bears in any state to that of its husbandmen, is the proportion of its unsound to its healthy parts, and is a good-enough barometer whereby to measure its degree of corruption. . . . for the general operations of manufacture, let our work-shops remain in Europe. It is better to carry provisions and materials to workmen there, than bring them to the provisions and materials, and with them their manners and principles. . . . It is the manners and spirit of a people which preserves a republic in vigour.[32]

In this very passage, however, there is detectable some doubt as to how long America can resist being drawn into the vortex of world commerce and all its influences. A few pages earlier Jefferson warns:

From the conclusion of this war we shall be going down hill. It will not then be necessary to resort every moment to the people for support. They will be forgotten, therefore, and their rights disregarded. They will forget themselves, but in the sole faculty of making money, and will never think of uniting to effect a due respect for their rights. The shackles, therefore, which shall not be knocked off at the conclusion of this war, will remain on us long, will be made heavier and heavier, till our rights shall revive or expire in convulsion.[33]

And Jefferson seems himself to bow to—nay, to embrace—the very forces of which he warns. He declares that "our interest will be to throw open the doors of commerce, and to knock off all its shackles, giving perfect freedom to all persons for the vent of whatever they may chuse to bring into our ports, and asking the same in theirs."[34] The truth is, Jefferson never very seriously opposed, he in fact fostered—sometimes with enthusiasm—an ever more prosperous, growth-oriented economy. Moreover, in his query on "Manners," Jefferson levels the severest attack upon the moral effects of slavery, a key part of the foundation of the agrarian South and an even more essential foundation of the great agrarian republics of antiquity.[35] Jefferson abhorred land speculators of the vulgar sort; but throughout his life he was relentless in campaigning against all relics of the laws of primogeniture and entail that had in past ages strictly limited the possibilities for speculation, rootlessness, acquisitiveness, and growth on the part of the landed aristocracy and gentry. No doubt the inegalitarian institutions of the old feudal and classical orders limited access to the land; but can access to land, and to prosperity from land, be opened up without introducing the powerful commercial forces that erode and corrode the yeoman spirit in which Jefferson placed so much trust? In short, are Jefferson's deep reservations against the commercial republic as envisaged by other Founders ultimately coherent or thought through?[36]

Still, Jefferson's concern about the ultimate fate of what he perceived to be the rural backbone of the republic dimly reflects a great theme of classical republicanism, a theme closely tied to that of virtue. Classical republicanism tended to favor, not farmers simply, as does Jefferson, but that minority among farmers which lives close enough to urban centers to attend regularly and partake in the political, religious, and artistic gatherings of the *polis*. More particularly, the classical spokesmen recommend recruiting the leadership of republics from a portion of what may be termed the landed gentry: they have in mind those gentlemen-farmers, living in the close vicinity of the city, who have, on the one hand, enough wealth to enjoy and appreciate leisure, and the educational benefits and variety of experience leisure can bring, but who, on the other hand, possess wealth of such a character as does not conduct easily to luxurious idleness, speculation, rapid growth, and easy mobility. Such men tend to be tied to a less acquisitive, more stable, and more patriotic or public-spirited existence than are the commercial wealthy or the large plantation owners. They can be led toward lives of steady ambition and public service, mingled with retreats to periods of reflection and preoccupation with the arts. The *Federalist,* in contrast, while it certainly expects to find rural interest represented by rural men in the national legislature, is largely indifferent to whether these rural representatives "happen to be men of large fortunes, or of moderate property, or of no property at all" (35:215); and, what is of much greater significance, the *Federalist* by no means seeks to give the rural or landed interest an especially favored position. Instead, Publius looks to a very different source for the recruitment of a major portion of the new republic's leadership, a source whose qualities are more congruent with the qualities we have seen that Publius seeks to cultivate in the citizenry at large. Lawyers and merchants (the latter of whom Publius calls "the natural patrons and friends" of the "manufacturers") (214) are to form the chief elements in the new national representative government.

This does not mean that Publius thinks the new republic can get along without patriotic politicians and at least some statesmen of rare strengths—leaders possessed of unusual "fortitude" of spirit, long-range ambition, and farsighted practical "wisdom."[37] But the *Federalist* has remarkably little to say about how such men will be cultivated and formed.[38] On the whole, the expectation seems to be that such men will arise spontaneously, without special efforts of education, character formation, and encouragement. In their arguments against the Antifederalists, the Federalists contend that vigorous, effective, and large-scale government will attract the most talented and help expose the incompetent or venal.[39] Yet Publius also warns against counting on the availability of "enlightened statesmen" (10:80): part of the genius of the new system is its devising of institutional mechanisms to channel, balance, and exploit petty passions in such a way as to obviate the need for constant reliance on noble impulses. Publius, in fact, has some considerable doubt as to whether statesmen can be trusted to be devoted to virtue or the common good, without external guards and constraints. Still, in this regard Publius is not nearly as extreme, and does not break so radically with the classical tradition, as do Jefferson and many or most of the Antifederalists:

> As there is a degree of depravity in mankind which requires a
> certain degree of circumspection and distrust, so there are other

qualities in human nature which justify a certain portion of esteem and confidence. Republican government presupposes the existence of these qualities in a higher degree than any other form.
Were the pictures which have been drawn by the political jeal-
ousy of some among us faithful likenesses of the human character, the inference would be that there is not sufficient virtue
among men for self-government. (55:346)[40]

Doubtless this is not an enthusiastic encomium to virtue. Publius acknowledges that "there are men who could neither be
distressed nor won into a sacrifice of their duty"; but he immediately adds that "this stern virtue is the growth of few soils"
(73:441). Gerald Stourzh, in his *Alexander Hamilton and the Idea of
Republican Government,* has persuasively argued that Hamilton,
more than his other distinguished colleagues, looked with favor
and hope upon "the pursuit of greatness" in men of political
ambition: and it is Hamilton who provides, in *Federalist* No. 72,
the most revealing disclosure of Publius's inner thought on the
place of the moral virtues in the human heart. There Hamilton
speaks, in Machiavellian accents, of the "love of fame" as "the
ruling passion of the noblest minds" (437). The noblest men,
those who are presumably most familiar with the allure of the
moral virtues, are not ruled by the love of those virtues but by the
love of a reward they may bring.[41] No wonder, then, that a
sound regime, as the authors of the *Federalist* envisage it, will
trust less to the high moral quality of its leaders and more to an
institutional system that pits the leaders' competing selfish passions against one another:

> The aim of every political constitution is, or ought to be,
> first to obtain for rulers men who possess most wisdom to dis-
> cern, and most virtue to pursue, the common good of the soci-
> ety; and in the next place, to take the most effectual precautions
> for keeping them virtuous whilst they continue to hold their
> public trust. (57:350)

Ambition must be made to counteract ambition. The interest of
the man must be connected with the constitutional rights of the
place. It may be a reflection on human nature that such devices
should be necessary to control the abuses of government. But

what is government itself but the greatest of all reflections on human nature? . . .

This policy of supplying, by opposite and rival interests, the defect of better motives, might be traced through the whole system of human affairs, private as well as public. We see it particularly displayed in all the subordinate distributions of power, where the constant aim is to divide and arrange the several offices in such a manner as that each may be a check on the other—that the private interest of every individual may be a sentinel over the public rights. (51:322)[42]

The *Federalist* is the first work in the history of political philosophy to stress the virtue of "responsibility." When Publius speaks of "responsibility," however, he has in mind something very different from our contemporary notion. "Responsibility," in the *Federalist,* is a virtue not of men but of political institutions: it is the excellence of a system that guarantees that no statesman will be autonomous—that no political leader will be independent from the "censure" or the "punishment" of the "public" (63:383–84, 70:427–28, 77:461).[43] But we see then that Publius, by his notion of "responsibility," decisively prepares the way for our notion and its peculiar moral thrust. Today we tend to hear, especially among the educated young, that it is more important that one be "responsible," or that one "accept responsibility"—for personal "choices" or "choice of values"—than that one strive to partake, in some measure, of the classical moral virtues. One may be perfectly and fully "responsible" as an "individual," rather than as a "politician": in fact, responsibility, like its sister "authenticity," tends to be conceived as an excellence of the "free" or "liberated" individual, unchained from any inescapable ties to or involvement in family and country. The classical virtues, in contrast, are grounded in experience of and admiration for the rare excellences of rule exhibited by superior men. The classical virtues are centered on the practical wisdom of the *paterfamilias,* the statesman, and finally the "lawgiver" in the most comprehensive sense. Our Founding *Fathers* themselves exemplify such superiority;[44] but their teachings, as exemplified by the *Federalist* and its new virtue of "responsibility," helped begin the historical process whereby emulation of anything like Plutarchean heroism has tended more and more to disappear from all but the reliquaries of American life.

THOMAS L. PANGLE

One can imagine the questions concerning virtue that might
have been addressed to the framers by Plato, Aristotle, Cicero, or
Plutarch. "You avow your dependence on some version—however
altered or truncated—of what we called 'the virtues'; but does
your new order adequately cultivate even this modified version?
Can virtue in any form grow in a regime which regards virtue as a
means rather than as an end—or does virtue not begin to wither
when it is so conceived?"

A survey of the chief moral-educative devices advocated by the
classical republican tradition reveals that most are neglected in the
American system. The Constitution imposes minimal qualifications for holding high legislative or executive office—and no qualifications whatsoever for holding high judicial office. The Federalists would doubtless respond by stressing the filtering effect of
elective representative government (36:217; 57:350–52)—but is
popular election, however limited and channelled by institutional
arrangements, an adequate selector of political excellence? Titles of
nobility, the traditional reward and public manifestation of respect
for outstanding merit, are not merely rendered nonhereditary, as
some had suggested—they are altogether prohibited. Partly as a
result, there is no equivalent of the English House of Lords to serve
as an antidemocratic blend in a truly mixed regime. Although
Madison, in a letter to Jefferson dated October 24, 1787, termed
the United States Senate the "great anchor of the government," and
was well aware that "history informs us of no long-lived republic
which had not a senate" (63:385), there is in fact no true "*senato-
rial*" branch or element in the national government: there is no
council of elders, such as the classics thought essential in order to
insure the presence in government of men who possess economic
and political independence as well as the wisdom of experience and
the phlegmatic spirit of the aged.[45]

Some notable efforts that were made at the Constitutional
Convention to introduce elements of a distinctly classical concern
for virtue met with no success. Benjamin Franklin attempted, on
June 2, to argue that public servants in the executive branch
should receive no salaries, but only honor as recompense: "in all
cases of public service the less the profit the greater the honor."
As models for the bureaucracy, Franklin adduced Quaker commit-
teemen, and the high Sheriff in England, an office "well executed,
and usually by some of the principal Gentlemen of the County."

Regarding the office of chief executive, Franklin pointed gracefully to the chairman of the Convention, George Washington, who executed the office of commander-in-chief "for eight years together without the smallest salary." Franklin then asked (and answered) rhetorically, "And shall we doubt finding three or four men in all the U. States, with public spirit enough to bear sitting in peaceful Council for perhaps an equal term, merely to preside over our civil concerns, and see that our laws are duly executed[?]. Sir, I have a better opinion of our country." This speech and proposal, Madison reports, "was treated with great respect, but rather for the author of it than from any apparent conviction of its expediency or practicability."[46]

George Mason moved on August 20 that Congress be given the power to enact "sumptuary laws" (i.e., laws that forbid and penalize conspicuous consumption, luxury, and public displays of self-indulgence), on the ground that "no Government can be maintained unless the manners be made consonant to it." Mason noted the objection to sumptuary laws—"that they were contrary to nature"—and replied that this "was a vulgar error: the love of distinction it is true is natural; but the object of sumptuary laws is not to extinguish this principle but to give it a proper direction." After a brief discussion, with Ellsworth, Morris, and Gerry speaking in opposition, the motion failed, although Mason gained the support of three states out of eleven voting, even without the backing of his own state, Virginia. Mason stubbornly returned to the good fight, or to a more commercial version of it, at the outset of deliberations on September 13, this time moving "that a committee be appointed to report articles of Association for encouraging by the advice, the influence, and the example of the members of the Convention, oecomony frugality and American manufactures." This motion was adopted, and a committee was immediately appointed. The committee, however, made no report, and neither this motion nor the committee's appointment were recorded in the official journal.[47]

It is striking to note how slow the *Federalist* is to take advantage even of those opportunities for civic education that offer themselves. For example, when Publius discusses trial by jury in *Federalist* No. 83, he does so without any reference to the educative or edifying effect of the institution. Similarly, the elaborate discussion of military service, in Nos. 24 through 29, and No.

46, treats such service as an unfortunate necessity rather than as the crucial moral training ground for courage, solidarity, and discipline—the light in which the citizen army was viewed in the Aristotelian tradition, and in which it continued to be viewed by many contemporary Americans. Publius's understanding of the kind of universal military service appropriate to Americans is made clear in the following passage:

> To oblige the great body of the yeomanry and of the other classes of the citizens to be under arms for the purpose of going through military exercises and evolutions, as often as might be necessary to acquire the degree of perfection which would entitle them to the character of a well-regulated militia, would be a real grievance to the people and a serious public inconvenience and loss. It would form an annual deduction from the productive labor of the country to an amount which, calculating upon the present numbers of the people, would not fall far short of a million pounds. To attempt a thing which would abridge the mass of labor and industry to so considerable an extent would be unwise . . . Little more can reasonably be aimed at with respect to the people at large than to have them properly armed and equipped. (29:184–85)

Most revealing and important of all, the Constitution prohibits the establishment of any civil religion, and thus opens the way to fragmentation of faith and disintegration of shared religious tradition—something that had always previously been held to be the very backbone of republican fraternity.[48]

It is often said that the Founders, or at least some of them, were looking to the political and religious life of the states to provide the missing direct encouragement for moral edification. As our earlier references to the Massachusetts Constitution of 1780 illustrate, there is considerable plausibility to this surmise: one might add that the state militias were expected to continue to imbue citizens with something of the waspish spirit of the revolutionary warrior (46:299; 25:166).[49] Yet, a reading of the debates at the Convention leaves one amazed at how little reference there is to any such positive role for state and local government. In fact, in the case of the leading Federalists, and especially in the case of Madison, there is strong evidence of lively foreboding as regards some of the likely consequences of an independent and vigorous religious and political life in the states. In the Constitutional Convention, Madison repeatedly, almost desperately, insisted (and without success) that the national legislature should have an absolute veto power over any and all state legislation. He explained his reasons at length in his letter to Jefferson of October 24, 1787, and an excerpt conveys the tone:

> It may be said that the Judicial authority under our new system will keep the States within their proper limits, and supply the place of a negative on their laws. The answer is, that it is more convenient to prevent the passage of a law, than to declare it void after it is passed; that this will be particularly the case, where the law aggrieves individuals, who may be unable to support an appeal [against] a State to the supreme Judiciary; that a State which would violate the Legislative rights of the Union, would not be very ready to obey a Judicial decree in support of them . . .
>   . . . A constitutional negative on the laws of the States seems equally necessary to secure individuals [against] encroachments on their rights. The mutability of the laws of the States is found to be a serious evil. The injustice of them has been so frequent and so flagrant as to alarm the most steadfast friends of Republicanism. I am persuaded I do not err in saying that the evils issuing from these sources contributed more to that uneasiness which produced the Convention, and prepared the public mind for a general reform, than those which accrued to our national character and interest from the inadequacy of the Confederation to its immediate objects.[50]

There is indeed one aspect of the new political system with regard to which the founding generation of statesmen did show, in their practice at least, a strong concern for encouraging and rewarding gentlemanliness of an older, aristocratic sort. As Leonard White has shown in his history of the American civil service, from the beginning there was established in the bureaucracy a strong tradition which maintained itself even after the replacement of the original Federalist party by the Jeffersonian Democratic party:

> The continuation of Federalist methods of administration was natural, if not inevitable, and could be traced at almost every point. . . . One circumstance of special importance was the un-

THOMAS L. PANGLE

interrupted control of government and the administrative system after 1801 by gentlemen. . . . Beneath the political shift that Jefferson emphasized so greatly was a solid and unchanged official substructure. . . . The concept of a gentleman was drawn from Elizabethan England. Its central theme was virtue, which was understood to connote justice, prudence, temperance, fortitude, courtesy, and liberality. . . . Virginia was governed by the landholding gentry. Other states also were governed by persons drawn from the well-to-do, educated classes. The Federalist view of a gentleman put emphasis upon wealth and social position; Jefferson, however, talked and wrote about the *natural* gentleman. Most Federalists would have accepted John Adams' description of a gentleman in his *Defense of the Constitutions*: "By gentlemen are not meant the rich or the poor, the high-born or the low-born, . . . but all those who have received a liberal education. . . . We must, nevertheless, remember that *generally* those who are rich, and descended from families in public life, will have the best education."[51]

It is not surprising to find that this crucial relic of a classical "mixed regime," having little if any grounding in the Constitution, barely survived the demise of the founding generation:

The great debate over the removal power in 1789 had involved constitutional questions and related to the executive power. The new debate that opened in 1829 over the removal power was primarily concerned with the political and administrative consequences of its use to reward party workers. The theoretical defense of rotation was based upon attachment to democracy. . . . the formal and official defense of rotation was stated by Andrew Jackson in his first annual message: "The duties of all public officers are, or at least admit of being made, so plain and simple that men of intelligence may readily qualify themselves for their performance. . . . In a country where offices are created solely for the benefit of the people no one man has any more intrinsic right to official station than another." The elderly Madison privately condemned the practice of rotation (August 29, 1834): "the principle . . . could not fail to degrade any Administration."

One consequence of the election of 1828 was to terminate the quasi-monopoly of officeholding enjoyed by the class of gentle-

132

men who had been called to official positions since the foundation of the Republic. Officeholders tended now to be drawn
from the ranks of active politicians, a class that had its own
merit in some important respects, but one that did not serve to
elevate public morality.[52]

The Founders, for all their sobriety, were seized by a hope that
would have appeared, from the perspective of the previous or
classical tradition of republicanism, to be truly extraordinary in
its boldness: an acquisitive, and radically permissive or "individualistic" society (to use the term Tocqueville introduced), which
treats virtue as at most a noble means, is supposed to continue to
produce sufficient virtue in the citizenry, and enough leaders of
outstanding virtue, to maintain uncorrupted the institutions of a
massive, extended republic. The classic thinkers would surely not
have been surprised by the continuing uneasiness, among some of
the principal Founders, over the feebleness of civic education in
the new order. Jefferson's proposed educational reforms for the
people of the state of Virginia; Washington's (and others') propos-
als for a national university to train political leaders and create a
higher civil service, a proposal Jefferson refocused in his plans for
the University of Virginia; the concern we have discussed, for the
preservation of some spirit of old-fashioned gentlemanliness in
the bureaucracy or national administration; the earnest attempt
on the part of federal judges to instruct their circuit juries not
only about legal technicalities and the case at hand but more
generally about the principles of free government;[53] the append-
ing of a Bill of Rights to the Constitution, in part because the
Antifederalists insisted on it as an essential vehicle for educating
present and future generations of young Americans: all these are
symptomatic attempts to fill the perceived gap. But whether
these measures are or ever could be adequate to the task of producing great statesmen and a virtuous citizenry remains a pressing
and a doubtful question—a question which casts a faint shadow
over the celebration of our Constitutional Bicentennial.

Let James Wilson, from his lecture inaugurating the first
American Law School, in 1790, have the final word.

> I have been zealous—I hope I have not been altogether
> unsuccessful—in contributing the best of my endeavors towards

forming a system of government; I shall rise in importance, if I can be equally successful—I will not be less zealous—in contributing the best of my endeavors towards forming a system of education likewise, in the United States. I shall rise in importance, because I shall rise in usefulness. What are laws without manners? How can manners be formed, but by a proper education? The ancient wisdom of the best times did always make a just complaint, that states were too busy with their laws; and too negligent in point of education.[54]

Notes

1. See Jonathan Elliot, ed., *The Debates in the Several State Conventions, on the Adoption of the Federal Constitution,* 6 vols. (New York: Burt Franklin, 1968).

2. Douglas Adair, *Fame and the Founding Fathers* (New York: W.W. Norton, 1974), 15–16, 272–85.

3. Paul L. Ford, ed., *Pamphlets on the Constitution of the United States, Published During Its Discussion by the People, 1787–88* (1888; reprint, New York: Burt Franklin, 1971), 59. See Herbert J. Storing, *What the Anti-Federalists Were For* (Chicago: University of Chicago Press, 1981), 46–47. Cf. Gordon S. Wood, *The Creation of the American Republic 1776–1787* (New York: W. W. Norton, 1972), 610–12. Wood's discussion is marred by a not-uncharacteristic lack of precision, or a willingness to slip from one to another rather impressionistic interpretation of the same document. Wood at first refers to Webster's remarkable pronouncement as exemplary of a clear general tendency among Americans of the time (606–10); but then he soon severely qualifies this original impression: "such deprecations of public virtue were still sporadic and premature" (612).

4. "The 'Other' Federalist Papers: A Preliminary Sketch," *Political Science Reviewer* 6 (1976): 238–40.

5. Thomas L. Pangle, *Montesquieu's Philosophy of Liberalism* (Chicago: University of Chicago Press, 1973), esp. 48–106. See Gerald Stourzh's admirably succinct and clear discussion, in *Alexander Hamilton and the Idea of Republican Government* (Stanford: Stanford University Press, 1970), esp. 63–65. Stourzh is the only historian of the founding period I have encountered whose work evinces a sophisticated and lucid grasp of Montesquieu's political philosophy, above all Montesquieu's concept of "virtue." See also John Louis DeLolme's work, originally published in 1771, and widely cited during the founding period, with its attack on the principles and practice of ancient republicanism: *The Constitution of England* (London: Henry G. Bohn, 1853), esp. bk. 2, sec. 1, 141–47; sec. 5, 169–77; sec. 21, 339–40.

6. This crucial aspect of classical political theory is missed or obscured in Harry V. Jaffa's generally helpful essay, "The Virtue of a Nation of Cities: On the Jeffersonian Paradoxes," in *The Conditions of Freedom* (Baltimore: Johns Hopkins University Press, 1975), 99–110. See esp. 108–9 on Socrates' relation to Athens.

7. The movement of thought is presented most vividly in the dialogue between the Athenian Stranger and Megillus and Kleinias in Plato's *Laws,* esp. bks. 1–3 and 7; the same dialectical criticism can be seen in a characteristically less dramatic form in Aristotle's *Politics,* bks. 7–8.

8. See esp. Aristotle *Ethics* 3.8.

9. Plato *Republic* 430C.

135

10. Plato *Laws* 643b–47c.

11. Montesquieu, *The Spirit of the Laws,* trans. Thomas Nugent, 2 vols. (New York: D. Appleton, 1900), bk. 3, chaps. 3, 5–8.

12. Ibid., esp. bk. 4, chap. 2.

13. See Jefferson's letters to John Adams, Oct. 28, 1813 and Oct. 14, 1816 in Lester J. Cappon, ed., *The Adams-Jefferson Letters,* 2 vols. (Chapel Hill: University of North Carolina Press, 1959), 2:387–92, 490–93; to Thomas Law, June 13, 1814, in Adrienne Koch and William Peden, eds., *The Life and Selected Writings of Thomas Jefferson* (New York: Random House, The Modern Library, 1944), 636–40; and to William Short, Oct. 31, 1819, ibid., 693–97. Cf. Harvey C. Mansfield, Jr., "Thomas Jefferson," in *American Political Thought: The Philosophic Dimensions of American Statesmanship,* ed. Morton Frisch and Richard Stevens (New York: Charles Scribner's Sons, 1971), 39–40, 50. Contrast, with Jefferson's formulations in his letters, the ambiguous remarks of John Adams, "Thoughts on Government," in *The Political Writings of John Adams,* ed. George A. Peek, Jr. (Indianapolis: Bobbs-Merrill, 1954), 85: "the form of government which communicates ease, comfort, security, or, in one word, happiness to the greatest number of persons and in the greatest degree is best. All sober inquirers after truth, ancient and modern, pagan and Christian, have declared that the happiness of man, as well as his dignity, *consists* in virtue" (emphasis added). Compare the status of virtue in the Massachusetts Constitution of 1780, Part 1 (Declaration of Rights), Art. 18 (which Adams had a prominent role in drawing up): "Piety, justice, moderation, temperance, industry, and frugality, are absolutely necessary to preserve the advantages of liberty."

14. Randolph G. Adams, ed., *Selected Political Essays of James Wilson* (New York: Alfred A. Knopf, 1930), 210, 272, 275, 278, 285. See, in addition, Robert G. McCloskey, ed., *The Works of James Wilson,* 2 vols. (Cambridge: Harvard University Press, 1967), 238–39, 241–42, 284, 587, 598, and esp. 608.

15. In their admiration for the figure of George Washington, thoughtful Americans of the founding period come closest to a reinvigoration of the classical posture toward virtue; yet even or precisely here can be seen the striking contrast in tone. See Thomas Jefferson, "The Character of George Washington," in Koch and Peden, *Life and Writings of Thomas Jefferson,* 173–76; and Robert Faulkner's illuminating discussion of John Marshall's biography of Washington in *The Jurisprudence of John Marshall* (Princeton: Princeton University Press, 1968), 124–33. See also Fred Baumann's penetrating discussion in "A Toga for Washington," *The New Criterion* 2 (April 1984): 82–88 (Review of Garry Wills, *Cincinnatus: George Washington and the Enlightenment*).

16. *A Defense of the Constitutions of Government of the United States of America against the attack of M. Turgot, in his letter to Dr. Price, dated the twenty-second of March, 1778,* in George A. Peek, ed., *Political Writings of John Adams* (Indianapolis: Bobbs-Merrill, 1954), 116–18; cf. *Federalist Papers* 38:231–33.

17. Oscar and Mary F. Handlin, eds., "Introduction," in *The Popular Sources of Political Authority: Documents on the Massachusetts Constitution of 1780* (Cambridge: Harvard University Press, 1966), 29–33. Cf. John T. Agresto, "Liberty, Virtue, and Republicanism: 1776–1787," *Review of Politics* 39 (1977): 503. Madison's (and Jefferson's) estimation of the true place and importance of religious disputation seems revealed by Madison's remarkable statement in his private letter to Jefferson, Oct. 24, 1787: "However erroneous or ridiculous these [religious] grounds of dissension and faction may appear to the enlightened Statesman, or the benevolent Philosopher, the bulk of mankind who are neither Statesmen nor Philosophers, will continue to view them in a different light." See Robert A. Rutland et al., eds., *The Papers of James Madison,* 13 vols. (Chicago: University of Chicago Press, 1962), 10:213. Some of the Founders may well have thought or hoped that

religious toleration would lead to a vigorous diversity of religious viewpoints and argumentation; Madison, while not going this far, nonetheless claimed that toleration had strengthened religion in Virginia (see letters to Edward Everett, Mar. 19, 1823, and to Rev. Adams in 1832, in Gaillard Hunt, ed., *Writings of James Madison,* 9 vols. [New York: G. P. Putnam's Sons, 1900–10], 9:127, 485–87). The aged Jefferson, on the contrary, in a letter he stressed was confidential to James Smith, Dec. 8, 1822, expressed his "confident expectation" that "the present generation will see Unitarianism become the general religion of the United States." For an anticipation of such a view, consider Jefferson's advice to a young man whose education he was advising (letter to Peter Carr, Aug. 10, 1787), as well as his letters to Benjamin Rush, Apr. 21, 1803 and John Adams, Aug. 22, 1813. See Koch and Peden, *Life and Writings of Thomas Jefferson,* 431–33, 566–70, 703–4; Cappon, *The Adams-Jefferson Letters,* 2:368–69. See Jefferson's remarkable but less bold public statement in *Notes on the State of Virginia,* Query 17. Cf. Mansfield, "Thomas Jefferson," 28–29. Jaffa rather overstates the case, overlooking Jefferson's prudent rhetorical reserve, when he calls Jefferson "an inveterate denier of both the old rationalism and the old revelation." ("Virtue of a Nation of Cities," 101 [full citation at note 6]). In his letter to Adams of Aug. 22, 1813, Jefferson remarks, "You will be sensible how much interest I take in keeping myself clear of religious disputes before the public." In the letter to Rush, Apr. 21, 1803, he declares, "I am moreover averse to the communication of my religious tenets to the public."

For an excellent presentation of the Antifederalists' reservations against the Constitution on the ground of religion, see Storing, *What the Anti-Federalists Were For,* 22–23 [full citation at note 3]. For a vigorous and clear statement of the older view as to the relation between the "spirit of religion" and the "spirit of a gentleman," see Edmond Burke, "Reflections on the Revolution in France," 2:351–52, and "Letters on a Regicide Peace," 5:214, in *Works* (London: Henry G. Bohn, 1855).

18. Plutarch, "Life of Lycurgus," in *Plutarch's Lives,* trans. J. and W. Langhorne, 6 vols. (London: Sharpe & Son, 1819), 1:136.

19. See Max Farrand, ed., *The Records of the Federal Convention of 1787,* 4 vols. (New Haven: Yale University Press, 1966), 2:325, n.616; cf. Kenneth Silverman, *A Cultural History of the American Revolution* (Toronto: Fitzhenry and Whiteside, 1976), 574.

20. U.S. Constitution, Art. 1, Sec. 8, clause 8; cf. *The Federalist,* 43:271–72.

21. See Ralph Lerner, "Commerce and Character: The Anglo-American as New-Model Man," *William and Mary Quarterly* 36 (1979): 3–26.

22. See, in addition to 3:45, 11:91, 37:224, 43:280, 78:470, and 85:522, the emphatic references to moderation at the beginning and ending of the *Federalist*—1:34 and 85:527; cf. the essay of David Hume referred to in the latter passage ("Of the Rise and Progress of the Arts and Sciences") as well as "Of Refinement in the Arts," "Of the Coalition of Parties," and "Of the Protestant Succession," in *Essays Moral, Political, and Literary,* ed. Eugene Miller (Indianapolis: Liberty Press, 1985), 15, 25, 27, 53, 63, 271–72, 279, 414, 500, 510, 612; David Hume, *An Enquiry Concerning the Principles of Morals* (Oxford: Clarendon Press, 1955), sec. 9, pt. 1, 270. See Montesquieu, *The Spirit of the Laws,* esp. bk. 3, chap. 4; bk. 5, chap. 8; bk. 6, chaps. 1, 2, 9, 16, 19; bk. 22, chap. 22 (last page); and, above all, Montesquieu's statement of the intention of *The Spirit of the Laws* as a whole—bk. 29, chap. 1. On the intimate link between commerce and softness, see the *Federalist,* 6:56–57, and Montesquieu, *The Spirit of the Laws,* bk. 20, chap. 1: "Commerce cures destructive prejudices; and it is almost a general rule, that wherever there is found commerce, there are soft manners and morals, and that wherever there are soft manners and morals, there is found commerce. . . . It can be said that the laws of commerce perfect the manners and morals, in the same proportion that these same laws destroy

manners and morals. Commerce corrupts pure manners and morals: this was the subject of the complaints of Plato; it polishes and softens barbarian manners and morals, as we are seeing every day" (my translation). Cf. Pangle, *Montesquieu's Philosophy of Liberalism*, chap. 7.

23. Cf. David F. Epstein, *The Political Theory of the Federalist* (Chicago: University of Chicago Press, 1984), 60, 62, 64–65, 66, 83, 85–88, 92–95, 144–45, 162–63. I am not convinced, however, that Madison maintains so strict a distinction between the terms and conceptions "public [or common] good" and "justice" as Epstein claims.

24. On a very qualified deference, see 63:384; on reverence for law, see 25:167, 17:120, and Madison's letter to Jefferson, Feb. 4, 1790, in response to a letter from Jefferson, Sept. 6, 1789, in Marvin Meyers, ed., *The Mind of the Founder* (Indianapolis: Bobbs-Merrill, 1973), 229–34.

25. Adams, *Political Essays of James Wilson*, 186, 189–90.

26. Cf. Hamilton in 28:180–81.

27. Epstein, *Political Theory of the Federalist*, 193–97.

28. See Lerner, "Commerce and Character," 15–16 and 19–20.

29. Cf. "The spirit of enterprise, which characterizes the commercial part of America" (7:63), and "That unequaled spirit of enterprise, which signalizes the genius of the American merchants" (11:88).

30. David Hume, "Of Commerce," in *Essays*, 263. Quoted and discussed in Lerner, "Commerce and Character," 13. Cf. Hume's *Enquiry Concerning the Principles of Morals*, sec. 6, pt. 2, 249.

31. See Storing, *What the Anti-Federalists Were For*, 45–46, and the extensive references there.

32. Query 19; contrast *The Federalist*, 12:91–92.

33. Query 17.

34. Query 22.

35. Query 18.

36. "All the world is becoming commercial. Was it practicable to keep our new empire separated from them we might indulge ourselves in speculating whether commerce contributes to the happiness of mankind. But we cannot separate ourselves from them. Our citizens have had too full a taste of the comforts furnished by the arts & manufactures to be debarred the use of them. We must then in our defense endeavor to share as large a portion as we can of this modern source of wealth and power." Letter to George Washington, Mar. 15, 1784, in Thomas Jefferson, *Writings*, ed. Merrill Peterson (New York: Literary Classics of America, 1984), 787–88; cf. letters to John Jay, Aug. 23, 1785 and G. K. Hogendorp, Oct. 13, 1785, in Koch and Peden, *Life and Writings of Thomas Jefferson*, 377–78, 384–85. See Lerner, "Commerce and Character," 19, n. 46; Agresto, "Liberty, Virtue and Republicanism," 492–96; Lance Banning, *The Jeffersonian Persuasion* (Ithaca: Cornell University Press, 1978), 204–5, 300–301, and the letters discussed there. Joyce Appleby has quite properly questioned the fashionable tendency, represented by Banning and derived from Pocock, to ascribe to Jefferson a "classical republicanism" that can be traced to Aristotle by way of Harrington and Machiavelli. However, in her attempt to locate Jefferson firmly within emerging "Capitalism," Appleby errs in the opposite direction. Her claim that "Jefferson had freed himself from worries about the moral fiber of his countrymen" flies in the face of the textual evidence quoted above: see "What Is Still American in the Political Philosophy of Thomas Jefferson?" *William and Mary Quarterly* 39 (1982): 287–309 (quote from 293); cf. also Appleby, "Commercial Farming and the 'Agrarian Myth' in the Early Republic," *Journal of American History* 68 (1982): 833–49.

Similarly excessive corrective zeal marks John P. Diggins's assertion that Jefferson "identi-fied happiness with property and material pleasure" instead of "political ideals that ap-pealed to man's higher nature." See *The Lost Soul of American Politics: Virtue, Self-Interest, and the Foundations of Liberalism* (New York: Basic Books, 1984), 5.

Harry Jaffa's discussion is better informed as regards the history of political philoso-phy, and though he may underestimate the extent to which Jefferson and his partisans were open to commercialism and manufacturing, he gives a most helpful capsule sum-mary of the Jeffersonian paradoxes and their historical fate or role in the development of the Jacksonian and the pro-slavery movements. I cannot, however, accept his quasi-Nietzschean interpretation of the role of slavery in the Greek city. I would deny that the view articulated in America by John Taylor's *Arator,* that slavery, or more particularly the "submission and flattery of slaves" is "a school of good manners and morals," or that "the degradation of one class of human beings may be desirable in order to elevate the charac-ters of another class" is "of the essence of the aristocratic republicanism of the ancient world," at least as that republicanism was articulated by Aristotle and Plato. See "The Virtue of a Nation of Cities," 100–106, and "Agrarian Virtue and Republican Freedom," in *Equality and Liberty* (New York: Oxford University Press, 1965), esp. 54–66.

37. See the *Federalist,* 55:346, 57:353, 64:395, 65:398, 68:414.

38. As for Jefferson, see Mansfield, "Thomas Jefferson," 38–40, 50.

39. See Storing, *What the Anti-Federalists Were For,* 41–47.

40. Cf. ibid., chap. 6; and, on Jefferson, see Stourzh, *Alexander Hamilton and the Idea of Republican Government,* 96–97 [full citation at note 5].

41. Contrast Diotima's speech to Socrates in Plato's *Symposium:* "I believe that they all do everything for the sake of immortal virtue *and also* for the sake of such a reputation, i.e., for fame in a good sense—and the better they are, the more is this the case; for they have an erotic love for the immortal" (208d7–e1: my trans.). See Adair, *Fame and the Founding Fathers,* 4–22, and esp. note 7: Adair argues convincingly (19) for the influence of Bacon in determining Jefferson's "modern" conception of the nature and status of fame; but Adair fails to perceive how profoundly the influence of Machiavelli has *transformed* Hamilton's "classical" (or better, "*neo*-classical") conception. Stourzh, *Alexander Hamilton and the Idea of Republican Government,* 101, 174ff., has supplemented Adair, arguing, as regards Hamil-ton, for the influence of Hume's essay, "Of the Dignity or Meanness of Human Nature."

42. Cf. Hume, "That Politics May be Reduced to a Science," in *Essays,* 15–16.

43. Cf. Adair, *Fame and the Founding Fathers,* 257.

44. Cf. ibid., 6–21; Stourzh, *Alexander Hamilton and the Idea of Republican Government,* 174ff.

45. See James Wilson, in McCloskey, *Works of James Wilson,* 314–15; Wood, *Creation of the American Republic,* 206–26, 237–55; Bernard Bailyn, *The Ideological Origins of the American Revolution* (Cambridge: Harvard University Press, 1967), 278–301; Martin Dia-mond, "The Federalist," in Frisch and Stevens, *American Political Thought,* 59 [full citation at note 13].

46. Farrand, *Federal Convention of 1787,* vol. 1, 81ff. For the later history of the debate over salaries in the executive branch, a debate fraught with important and complex implications for civic virtue, see Leonard White, "The Rule of Parsimony," in *The Federal-ists: A Study in Administrative History, 1789–1801* (New York: Macmillan, 1948), chap. 23, and *The Jeffersonians: A Study in Administrative History, 1801–1829* (New York: Macmillan, 1951), chap. 27.

47. Farrand, *Federal Convention of 1787,* 2:344, 606–7; cf. Montesquieu, *Spirit of the Laws,* bk. 7, chaps. 2–5.

48. Cf. "An Act for Establishing Religious Freedom, passed in the Assembly of Virginia, in the beginning of the year 1786" (printed as Appendix 3 to Jefferson's *Notes on the State of Virginia*, and authored by Jefferson): "our civil rights have no dependence on our religious opinions." Compare n. 17 above, and Storing, *What the Anti-Federalists Were For*, 22–23 [full citation at note 3].

49. For an extensive discussion of the complex and shifting attitude toward militias and arms during the founding period, see Robert E. Shalhope and Lawrence D. Cress, "The Second Amendment and the Right to Bear Arms: An Exchange," *Journal of American History* 71 (1984): 587–93, and the texts and literature to which they refer.

50. Rutland et al., *The Papers of James Madison*, 10:209–14; cf. 3–6, 16, 41–44, 64, 102–3, 135, 154, 205–6. Subsequent to ratification, when Madison led the movement on the floor of the House of Representatives to draw up a Bill of Rights as amendments to the Constitution, he tried hard—but of course failed—to insert prohibitions on the states similar to those eventually found or read into the Reconstruction amendments: "I wish, also, in revising the Constitution, we may throw into that section, which interdicts the abuse of certain powers in the State Legislatures, some other provisions of equal, if not greater importance than those already made. . . . I think there is more danger of those powers being abused by the State Governments than by the Government of the United States" (Speech in the House of Representatives, June 8, 1789, in Meyers, *The Mind of The Founder*, 225–26 [full citation at note 24]).

51. Leonard White, *The Jeffersonians*, 547–49; cf. chap. 24, esp. 356–68; idem, *The Federalists*, ch. 21 ("Fitness of Character—Public Service Ideals"), 22 ("Ideals and Practice"), and 25 ("Notes on Prestige"). Cf. Adair, *Fame and the Founding Fathers*, 304.

52. Leonard White, *The Jacksonians: A Study in Administrative History, 1829–1861* (New York: Macmillan, 1954), 316–17, 320–21, 418–19; cf. chaps. 16–18, esp. 316–24, 347, and chaps. 21–22, esp. 411–12, 430, and 552–53. For the subsequent history, see *The Republican Era: A Study in Administrative History, 1869–1901* (New York: Macmillan, 1958), chap. 13 ("The Battle for Reform"); and Leonard White, "The Senior Civil Service," *Public Administration Review* 15 (Autumn 1955): 4, discussing and advocating the Second Hoover Commission's proposal (ultimately rejected) to create within the American bureaucracy a "higher civil service" elite corps.

53. See Ralph Lerner, "The Supreme Court as Republican Schoolmaster," in *Supreme Court Review, 1967*, ed. Philip Kurland (Chicago: University of Chicago Press, 1967), 127–80.

54. Adams, *Political Essays of James Wilson*, 208.

VI

THE POLITICAL THEORY OF THE PROCEDURAL REPUBLIC

★

Michael J. Sandel

My aim is to connect a certain debate in political theory with a certain development in our political practice. The debate is the one between rights-based liberalism and its communitarian, or civic republican critics. The development is the advent in the United States of what might be called the "procedural republic," a public life animated by the rights-based liberal ethic. In the modern American welfare state, it seems, the liberal dimensions of our tradition have crowded out the republican dimensions, with adverse consequences for the democratic prospect and the legitimacy of the regime.

In this essay I first identify the liberal and civic republican theories at issue in contemporary political philosophy, and then employ these contrasting theories in an interpretation of the

Michael Sandel is an Associate Professor of Government at Harvard University.

141

American political condition. I hope ultimately to show that we can illuminate our political practice by identifying the contending political theories and self-images it embodies. This essay is a preliminary effort in that direction.

Liberals often take pride in defending what they oppose—pornography, for example, or unpopular views.[1] They say the state should not impose on its citizens a preferred way of life, but should leave them as free as possible to choose their own values and ends, consistent with a similar liberty for others. This commitment to freedom of choice requires liberals constantly to distinguish between permission and praise, between allowing a practice and endorsing it. It is one thing to allow pornography, they argue, something else to affirm it.

Conservatives sometimes exploit this distinction by ignoring it. They charge that those who would allow abortions favor abortion, that opponents of school prayer oppose prayer, that those who defend the rights of Communists sympathize with their cause. And in a pattern of argument familiar in our politics, liberals reply by invoking higher principles; it is not that they dislike pornography less, but rather that they value toleration, or freedom of choice, or fair procedures more.

But in contemporary debate, the liberal rejoinder seems increasingly fragile, its moral basis increasingly unclear. Why should toleration and freedom of choice prevail when other important values are also at stake? Too often the answer implies some version of moral relativism, the idea that it is wrong to "legislate morality" because all morality is merely subjective. "Who is to say what is literature and what is filth? That is a value judgement, and who's values should decide?"

Relativism usually appears less as a claim than as a question ("Who is to judge?"). But it is a question that can also be asked of the values that liberals defend. Toleration and freedom and fairness are values too, and they can hardly be defended by the claim that no values can be defended. So it is a mistake to affirm liberal values by arguing that all values are merely subjective. The relativist defense of liberalism is no defense at all.

What then, can be the moral basis of the higher principles the liberal invokes? Recent political philosophy has offered two main alternatives—one utilitarian, the other Kantian. The utilitarian view, following John Stuart Mill, defends liberal principles in the name of maximizing the general welfare. The state should not impose on its citizens a preferred way of life, even for their own good, because doing so will reduce the sum of human happiness, at least in the long run; better that people choose for themselves, even if, on occasion, they get it wrong. "The only freedom which deserves the name," writes Mill, "is that of pursuing our own good in our own way, so long as we do not attempt to deprive others of theirs, or impede their efforts to obtain it." He adds that his argument does not depend on any notion of abstract right, only on the principle of the greatest good for the greatest number. "I regard utility as the ultimate appeal on all ethical questions; but it must be utility in the largest sense, grounded on the permanent interests of man as a progressive being."[2]

Many objections have been raised against utilitarianism as a general doctrine of moral philosophy. Some have questioned the concept of utility, and the assumption that all human goods are in principle commensurable. Others have objected that by reducing all values to preferences and desires, utilitarians are unable to admit qualitative distinctions of worth, unable to distinguish noble desires from base ones. But most recent debate has focused on whether utilitarianism offers a convincing basis for liberal principles, including respect for individual rights.

In one respect, utilitarianism would seem well-suited to liberal purposes. Maximizing utility does not require judging people's values, only aggregating them. And the willingness to aggregate preferences without judging them suggests a tolerant spirit, even a democratic one. When people go to the polls, we count their votes whatever they are.

But the utilitarian calculus is not always as liberal as it first appears. If enough cheering Romans pack the Coliseum to watch the lion devour the Christian, the collective pleasure of the Romans will surely outweigh the pain of the Christian, intense though it be. Or if a big majority abhors a small religion and wants it banned, the balance of preferences will favor suppression, not toleration. Utilitarians sometimes defend individual rights on the grounds that respecting them now will serve utility in the long run. But this calculation is precarious and contingent. It hardly secures the liberal promise not to impose on some people the values of others. As the majority will is an inadequate instrument of liberal politics—by itself it fails to secure individual rights—so the utilitarian philosophy is an inadequate foundation for liberal principles.

The case against utilitarianism was made most powerfully by Kant. He argued that empirical principles, such as utility, were unfit to serve as basis for the moral law. A wholly instrumental defense of freedom and rights not only leaves rights vulnerable, but fails to respect the inherent dignity of persons. The utilitarian calculus treats people as means to the happiness of others, not as ends in themselves, worthy of respect.[3]

Contemporary liberals extend Kant's argument with the claim that utilitarianism fails to take seriously the distinction between persons. In seeking above all to maximize the general welfare, the utilitarian treats society as a whole as if it were a single person; it conflates our many and diverse desires into a single system of desires, and tries to maximize. It is indifferent to the distribution of satisfactions among persons, except insofar as this may affect the overall sum. But this fails to respect our plurality and distinctness. It uses some as means to the happiness of all, and so fails to respect each as an end in himself.

Modern-day Kantians reject the utilitarian approach in favor of an ethic that takes rights more seriously. In their view, certain rights are so fundamental that even the general welfare cannot override them. As John Rawls writes, "Each person possesses an inviolability founded on justice that even the welfare of society as a whole cannot override . . . the rights secured by justice are not subject to political bargaining or to the calculus of social interests."[4]

So Kantian liberals need an account of rights that does not depend on utilitarian considerations. More than this, they need an account that does not depend on any particular conception of the good, that does not presuppose the superiority of one way of life over others. Only a justification neutral about ends could preserve the liberal resolve not to favor any particular ends, or to impose on its citizens a preferred way of life.

But what sort of justification could this be? How is it possible to affirm certain liberties and rights as fundamental without embracing some vision of the good life, without endorsing some ends over others? It would seem we are back to the relativist predicament—to affirm liberal principles without embracing any particular ends.

The solution proposed by Kantian liberals is to draw a distinction between the "right" and the "good"—between a framework of basic rights and liberties, and the conceptions of the good that people may choose to pursue within that framework. It is one thing for the state to support a fair framework, they argue, but something else to affirm some particular ends. For example, it is one thing to defend the right to free speech so that people may be free to form their own opinions and choose their own ends, but something else to support it on the grounds that a life of political discussion is inherently worthier than a life unconcerned with public affairs, or on the grounds that free speech will increase the general welfare. Only the first defense is available on the Kantian view, resting as it does on the ideal of a neutral framework.

Now the commitment to a framework neutral among ends can be seen as a kind of value—in this sense the Kantian liberal is no relativist—but this value consists precisely in its refusal to affirm a preferred way of life or conception of the good. For Kantian liberals, then, the right is prior to the good, and in two senses. First, individual rights cannot be sacrificed for the sake of the general good, and second, the principles of justice that specify these rights cannot be premised on any particular vision of the good life. What justifies the rights is not that they maximize the general welfare or otherwise promote the good, but rather that they comprise a fair framework within which individuals and groups can choose their own values and ends, consistent with a similar liberty for others.

Of course, proponents of the rights-based ethic notoriously disagree about what rights are fundamental, and about what political arrangements the ideal of the neutral framework requires. Egalitarian liberals support the welfare state, and favor a scheme of civil liberties together with certain social and economic rights—rights to welfare, education, health care, and so on. Libertarian liberals defend the market economy, and claim that redistributive policies violate people's rights; they favor a scheme of civil liberties combined with a strict regime of private property rights. But whether egalitarian or libertarian, rights-based liberalism begins with the claim that we are separate, individual persons, each with our own aims, interests, and conceptions of the good, and seeks a framework of rights that will enable us to realize our capacity as free moral agents, consistent with a similar liberty for others.

II

Within academic philosophy, the last decade or so has seen the ascendance of the rights-based ethic over the utilitarian one, owing in large part to the influence of John Rawls's important work, *A Theory of Justice*. In the debate between utilitarian and rights-based theories, the rights-based ethic has come to prevail. The legal philosopher H. L. A. Hart recently described the shift from "the old faith that some form of utilitarianism must capture the essence of political morality" to the new faith that "the truth must lie with a doctrine of basic human rights, protecting specific basic liberties and interests of individuals. . . . Whereas not so long ago great energy and much ingenuity of many philosophers were devoted to making some form of utilitarianism work, lately such energies and ingenuity have been devoted to the articulation of theories of basic rights."[5]

But in philosophy as in life, the new faith becomes the old orthodoxy before long. Even as it has come to prevail over its utilitarian rival, the rights-based ethic has recently faced a growing challenge from a different direction, from a view that gives fuller expression to the claims of citizenship and community than the liberal vision allows. Recalling the arguments of Hegel against Kant, the communitarian critics of modern liberalism question the claim for the priority of the right over the good, and the picture of the freely choosing individual it embodies. Following Aristotle, they argue that we cannot justify political arrangements without reference to common purposes and ends, and that we cannot conceive our personhood without reference to our role as citizens, and as participants in a common life.

This debate reflects two contrasting pictures of the self. The rights-based ethic, and the conception of the person it embodies, were shaped in large part in the encounter with utilitarianism. Where utilitarians conflate our many desires into a single system of desire, Kantians insist on the separateness of persons. Where the utilitarian self is simply defined as the sum of its desires, the Kantian self is a choosing self, independent of the desires and ends it may have at any moment. As Rawls writes, "The self is prior to the ends which are affirmed by it; even a dominant end must be chosen from among numerous possibilities."[6]

The priority of the self over its ends means I am never defined by my aims and attachments, but always capable of standing back to survey and assess and possibly to revise them. This is what it means to be a free and independent self, capable of choice. And this is the vision of the self that finds expression in the ideal of the state as a neutral framework. According to the rights-based ethic, it is precisely because we are essentially separate, independent selves that we need a neutral framework, a framework of rights that refuses to choose among competing purposes and ends. If the self is prior to its ends, then the right must be prior to the good.

Communitarian critics of rights-based liberalism say we cannot conceive ourselves as independent in this way, as bearers of selves wholly detached from our aims and attachments. They say that certain of our roles are partly constitutive of the persons were are—as citizens of a country, or members of a movement, or partisans of a cause. But if we are partly defined by the communities we inhabit, then we must also be implicated in the purposes and ends characteristic of those communities. As Alasdair MacIntyre writes, "what is good for me has to be the good for one who inhabits these roles."[7] Open-ended though it be, the story of my life is always embedded in the story of those communities from which I derive my identity—whether family or city, people or nation, party or cause. According to the communitarian view, these stories make a moral difference, not only a psychological one. They situate us in the world, and give our lives their moral particularity.

What is at stake for politics in the debate between unencumbered selves and situated ones? What are the practical differences between a politics of rights and a politics of the common good? On some issues, the two theories may produce different arguments for similar policies. For example, the civil rights movement of the 1960's might be justified by liberals in the name of human dignity and respect for persons, and by communitarians in the name of recognizing the full membership of fellow citizens wrongly excluded from the common life of the nation. And where liberals might support public education in hopes of equipping students to become autonomous individuals, capable of choosing their own ends and pursuing them effectively, communitarians might support public education in hopes of equipping students to become good citizens, capable of contributing meaningfully to public deliberations and pursuits.

On other issues, the two ethics might lead to different policies. Communitarians would be more likely than liberals to allow a town to ban pornographic bookstores, on the grounds that pornography offends its way of life and the values that sustain it. But a politics of civic virtue does not always part company with liberalism in favor of conservative policies. For example, communitarians would be more willing than some rights-oriented liberals to see states enact laws regulating plant closings, to protect their communities from the disruptive effects of capital mobility and sudden industrial change. More generally, where the liberal regards the expansion of individual rights and entitlements as unqualified moral and political progress, the communitarian is troubled by the tendency of liberal programs to displace politics from smaller forms of association to more comprehensive ones. Where libertarian liberals defend the private economy and egalitarian liberals defend the welfare state, communitarians worry about the concentration of power in both the corporate economy and the bureaucratic state, and the erosion of those intermediate forms of community that have at times sustained a more vital public life.

Liberals often argue that a politics of the common good, drawing as it must on particular loyalties, obligations, and traditions, opens the way to prejudice and intolerance. The modern nation-state is not the Athenian *polis*, they point out; the scale and diversity of modern life have rendered the Aristotelean political ethic nostalgic at best and dangerous at worst. Any attempt to govern by a vision of the good is likely to lead to a slippery slope of totalitarian temptations.

Communitarians reply that intolerance flourishes most where forms of life are dislocated, roots unsettled, traditions undone. In our day, the totalitarian impulse has sprung less from the convictions of confidently situated selves than from the confusions of atomized, dislocated, frustrated selves, at sea in a world where common meanings have lost their force. As Hannah Arendt has written, "What makes mass society so difficult to bear is not the number of people involved, or at least not primarily, but the fact that the world between them has lost its power to gather them together, to relate and to separate them."[8] Insofar as our public life has withered, our sense of common involvement diminished, we lie vulnerable to the mass politics of totalitarian solutions. So responds the party of the common good to the party of rights. If the party of the common good is right, our most pressing moral and political project is to revitalize those civic republican possibilities implicit in our tradition but fading in our time.

III

How might the contrast between the liberal and communitarian, or civic republican, theories we have been considering help illuminate our present political condition? We might begin by locating these theories in the political history of the American republic. Both the liberal and the republican conceptions have been present throughout, but in differing measure and with shifting importance. Broadly speaking, the republican strand was most evident from the time of the founding to the late nineteenth century; by the mid to late twentieth century, the liberal conception came increasingly to predominate, gradually crowding out republican dimensions. I shall try in this section to identify three moments in the transition from the republican to the liberal constitutional order: (1) the civic republic, (2) the national republic, and (3) the procedural republic.

CIVIC REPUBLIC

The ideological origins of American politics is the subject of lively and voluminous debate among intellectual historians. Some emphasize the Lockean liberal sources of American political thought, others the civic republican influences.[9] But beyond the question of who influenced the Founders' thought is the further question of what kind of political life they actually lived. It is clear that the assumptions embodied in the practice of eighteenth-century American politics, the ideas and institutions that together constitute the "civic republic," differ from those of the modern liberal political order in several respects. First, liberty in the civic republic was defined, not in opposition to democracy, as an individual's guarantee against what the majority might will, but as a function of democracy, of democratic institutions and dispersed power. In the eighteenth century, civil liberty referred not to a set of personal rights, in the sense of immunities, as in the modern "right to privacy," but, in Hamilton's words, "to a share in the government." Civil liberty was public, or political liberty, "equivalent to democracy or government by the people themselves." It was not primarily individual, but "the freedom of bodies politic, or States."[10]

Second, the terms of relation between the individual and the nation were not direct and unmediated, but indirect, mediated by decentralized forms of political association, participation, and allegiance. As Laurence Tribe points out, "it was largely through the preservation of boundaries between and among institutions that the rights of persons were to be secured."[11] Perhaps the most vivid constitutional expression of this fact is that the Bill of Rights did not apply to the states, and was not understood to create individual immunities from all government action. When Madison proposed, in 1789, a constitutional amendment providing that "no State shall infringe the equal rights of conscience, nor the freedom of speech or of the press, nor of the right of trial by jury in criminal cases," the liberal, rights-based ethic found its clearest early expression. But Madison's proposal was rejected by the Senate, and did not succeed until the Fourteenth Amendment was passed some seventy-nine years later.

Finally, the early republic was a place where the possibility of civic virtue was a live concern. Some saw civic virtue as essential to the preservation of liberty; others despaired of virtue, and sought to design institutions that could function without it.[12] But as Tocqueville found in his visit to the New England townships, public life functioned in part as an education in citizenship: "Town meetings are to liberty what primary schools are to science; they bring it within the people's reach, they teach men how to use and how to enjoy it. A nation may establish a free government, but without municipal institutions it cannot have the spirit of liberty."[13]

NATIONAL REPUBLIC

The transition to the national, and ultimately, the procedural republic, begins to unfold from the end of the Civil War to the turn of the century.[14] As national markets and large-scale enterprise displaced a decentralized economy, the decentralized political forms of the early republic became outmoded as well. If democracy was to survive, the concentration of economic power would have to be met by a similar concentration of political power. But the Progressives understood, or some of them did, that the success of democracy required more than the centralization of government; it also required the nationalization of politics. The primary form of political community had to be recast on a national scale. For Herbert Croly, writing in 1909, the "nationalizing of American political, economic, and social life" was "an essentially formative and enlightening political transformation." We would become more of a democracy only as we became "more of a nation . . . in ideas, in institutions, and in spirit."[15]

This nationalizing project would be consummated in the New Deal, but for the democratic tradition in America, the embrace of the nation was a decisive departure. From Jefferson to the populists, the party of democracy in American political debate had been, roughly speaking, the party of the provinces, of decentralized power, of small-town and small-scale America. And against them had stood the party of the nation—first Federalists, then Whigs, then the Republicans of Lincoln—a party that spoke for the consolidation of the union. It was thus the historic achievement of the New Deal to unite, in a single party and political program, what Samuel Beer has called "liberalism and the national idea."[16]

What matters for our purpose is that, in the twentieth century, liberalism made its peace with concentrated power. But it was understood at the start that the terms of this peace required a strong sense of national community, morally and politically, to underwrite the extended involvements of a modern industrial order. If a virtuous republic of small-scale, democratic communities was no longer a possibility, a national republic seemed democracy's next best hope. This was still, in principle at least, a politics of the common good. It looked to the nation, not as a neutral framework for the play of competing interests, but rather as a formative community, concerned to shape a common life suited to the scale of modern social and economic forms.

But by the mid-twentieth century, the national republic had run its course. Except for extraordinary moments, such as war, the nation proved too vast a scale across which to cultivate the

shared self-understandings necessary to community in the formative, or constitutive sense. And yet, given the scale of economic
and political life, there seemed no turning back. If so extended a
republic could not sustain a politics of the common good, a
different sort of legitimating ethic would have to be found. And
so the gradual shift, in our practices and institutions, from a
public philosophy of common purposes to one of fair procedures,
from the national republic to the procedural republic.

PROCEDURAL REPUBLIC

The procedural republic represents the triumph of a liberal
public philosophy over a republican one, with adverse consequences for democratic politics and the legitimacy of the regime.
It reverses the terms of relation between liberty and democracy,
transforms the relation of the individual and nation-state, and
tends to undercut the kind of community on which it nonetheless
depends. Liberty in the procedural republic is defined, not as a
function of democracy but in opposition to democracy, as an
individual's guarantee against what the majority might will. I am
free insofar as I am the bearer of rights, where rights are
trumps.[17] Unlike the liberty of the early republic, the modern
version permits—in fact even requires—concentrated power.
This has at least partly to do with the universalizing logic of
rights. Insofar as I have a right, whether to free speech or a
minimum income, its provision cannot be left to the vagaries of
local preferences but must be assured at the most comprehensive
level of political association. It cannot be one thing in New York
and another in Alabama. As rights and entitlements expand,
politics is therefore displaced from smaller forms of association
and relocated at the most universal form—in our case, the nation.
And even as politics flows to the nation, power shifts away from
democratic institutions (such as legislatures and political parties),
toward institutions designed to be insulated from democratic
pressures, and hence better equipped to dispense and defend individual rights (notably the judiciary and bureaucracy).

These institutional developments may begin to account for the
sense of powerlessness that the welfare state fails to address and in
some ways doubtless deepens. But it seems to me that a further
clue to our condition can be located in the vision of the unencum-

bered self that animates the liberal ethic. It is a striking feature of the welfare state that it offers a powerful promise of individual rights, and also demands of its citizens a high measure of mutual engagement. But the self-image that attends the rights cannot sustain the engagement. As bearers of rights, where rights are trumps, we think of ourselves as freely choosing, individual selves, unbound by obligations antecedent to rights, or to the agreements we make. And yet, as citizens of the procedural republic that secures these rights, we find ourselves implicated willy-nilly in a formidable array of dependencies and expectations we did not choose and increasingly reject.

In our public life, we are more entangled, but less attached, than ever before. It is as though the unencumbered self presupposed by the liberal ethic had begun to come true—less liberated than disempowered, entangled in a network of obligations and involvements unassociated with any act of will, and yet unmediated by those common identifications or expansive self-definitions that would make them tolerable. As the scale of social and political organization has become more comprehensive, the terms of our collective identity have become more fragmented, and the forms of political life have outrun the common purposes needed to sustain them.

Notes

1. In this and the following section, I draw on the introduction to *Liberalism and Its Critics,* ed. Michael J. Sandel (Oxford: Basil Blackwell, 1984).

2. John Stuart Mill, *On Liberty* (Garden City, N.Y.: Anchor Books, 1973), chap. 1.

3. See Immanuel Kant, *Groundwork of the Metaphysics of Morals,* trans. H. J. Paton (New York: Harper and Row, 1956), and "On The Common Saying: 'This May Be True In Theory, But It Does Not Apply In Practice,' " in *Kant's Political Writings,* ed. Hans Reiss (Cambridge: Cambridge University Press, 1970).

4. John Rawls, *A Theory of Justice* (Oxford: Oxford University Press, 1971), 3–4.

5. H. L. A. Hart, "Between Utility And Rights," in *The Idea of Freedom,* ed. Alan Ryan (Oxford: Oxford University Press, 1979), 77.

6. Rawls, *Theory of Justice,* 560.

7. Alasdair MacIntyre, *After Virtue* (Notre Dame: University of Notre Dame Press, 1981), 205.

8. Hannah Arendt, *The Human Condition* (Chicago: University of Chicago Press, 1958), 52–53.

9. For examples of the liberal view, see Louis Hartz, *The Liberal Tradition in America* (New York: Harcourt, Brace & Co., 1955), and more recently, Isaac Kramnick, "Republican Revisionism Revisited," *American Historical Review* 87 (1982): 629–64, and John Diggins, *The Lost Soul of American Politics* (New York: Basic Books, 1984). For examples of the republican view, see Bernard Bailyn, *The Ideological Origins of the American Revolution* (Cambridge: Harvard University Press, 1967), Gordon Wood, *The Creation of the American Republic, 1776–1787* (New York: Norton, 1969), and J. G. A. Pocock, *The Machiavellian Moment* (Princeton: Princeton University Press, 1975).

10. Wood, *Creation of the American Republic,* 24, 61.

11. Laurence Tribe, *American Constitutional Law* (Mineola, N.Y.: Foundation Press, 1978), 2–3.

12. See, for example, Madison's *Federalist* No. 51, and Herbert J. Storing, *What the Anti-Federalists Were For* (Chicago: University of Chicago Press, 1981), chap. 3.

13. Alexis de Tocqueville, *Democracy in America,* vol. 1, ed. Phillips Bradley (New York: Alfred A. Knopf, 1972), chap. 5.

14. In this and the following section, I have drawn from Michael J. Sandel, "The Procedural Republic and The Unencumbered Self," *Political Theory* 12 (1984): 81–96.

15. Herbert Croly, *The Promise of American Life* (Indianapolis: Bobbs-Merrill, 1965), 270–73.

16. Samuel Beer, "Liberalism and The National Idea," *The Public Interest* 5 (Fall 1966): 70–82.

17. See Ronald M. Dworkin, "Liberalism," in *Public and Private Morality*, ed. Stuart Hampshire (Cambridge: Cambridge University Press, 1978), 136.

Index

DATE DUE

DATE DUE			
OCT 05 '92			
NOV 1 '92			
	261-2500		Printed in USA